Sexuality and Our Faith

A Companion to

Our Whole Lives

Grades 7–9

Sexuality and Our Faith

A Companion to

Our Whole Lives

Grades 7–9

Rev. Makanah Elizabeth Morriss & Rev. Jory Agate
for the UUA

Rev. Lizann Bassham & Rev. Gordon J. Svoboda II
for the UCBHM

Judith A. Frediani
Developmental Editor

Unitarian Universalist Association
United Church Board for Homeland Ministries
BOSTON

The Sexuality Education Task Force Core Committee (1994–2000) is responsible for the development of the *Our Whole Lives* curricula and companion resources. Members have included:

Reverend Makanah Elizabeth Morriss (UUA), co-chair
Reverend Gordon J. Svoboda II (UCC), co-chair
Reverend Lena Breen (UUA), co-chair
Reverend Jory Agate (UUA)
Kathleen Carlin (UCC)
Dr. Duane Dowell (UUA)
Judith A. Frediani (UUA)
Sarah Gibb (UUA/UCC)
Jennifer Devine (UUA)
Reverend Patricia Hoertdoerfer (UUA)
Faith Adams Johnson (UCC)

In appreciation of Kathleen Carlin (January 13, 1939–September 20, 1996) who deepened our understanding of sexual justice and who enriched our committee with her presence and love.

ISBN 1-55896-395-2
978-1-55896-395-5

10 9 8 7 6 5 4
09 08 07

The United Church Board of Homeland Ministries has disincorporated since this book was published. For matters related to that publisher, please contact the *Our Whole Lives* consultant at the United Church of Christ, 700 Prospect Avenue, Cleveland, Ohio, 216/736-3718.

Curriculum Development Assistant *Dorothy M. Ellis*
Text Designer *Sandra Rigney*
Cover Designer *Isaac Stone*

Contents

Supporting Sexuality Education in Your Congregation viii

Unitarian Universalist Religious Supplement to
Our Whole Lives Sexuality Education for Grades 7-9

Introduction to the Unitarian Universalist Companion 3

UNIT ONE **Group Building and Examining Values** 9
Session 1 **Introduction to the Program** • Session 2 **Examining Values**

UNIT TWO **Sexuality and Body Awareness** 15
Session 3 **Sexual Language** • Session 4 **Anatomy and Physiology** •
Session 5 **Personal Concerns About Puberty**

UNIT THREE **Gender and Diversity** 23
Session 6 **Understanding Gender Roles** •
Session 7 **Disability and Other Diversity Issues**

UNIT FOUR **Sexual Orientation and Gender Identity** 29
Session 8 **Sexual Orientation** • Session 9 **Guest Panel** •
Session 10 **Gender Identity**

UNIT FIVE **Relationships** 39
Session 11 **Introduction to Relationships** • Session 12 **Relationship Skills** •
Session 13 **Thorny Issues in Friendship** • Session 14 **Dating and Lifetime Commitments**

UNIT SIX **Lovemaking** 49
Session 15 **Lovemaking Is More Than Sex** • Session 16 **Masturbation and Other Sexual Behaviors**

UNIT SEVEN **Preparing for Parenthood** 55

Session 17 **Conception, Planned Pregnancy, and Birth** •
Session 18 **Teenage Pregnancy**

UNIT EIGHT **Responsible Sexual Behavior** 61

Session 19 **Defining/Redefining Abstinence** • Session 20 **Contraception** •
Session 21 **Unintended Pregnancy Options** • Session 22 **Sexual Decisions**

UNIT NINE **Sexually Transmitted Diseases (STDs)** 71

Session 23 **STD Facts** • Session 24 **STD Prevention**

UNIT TEN **Abuse of Sexuality** 77

Session 25 **Recovering from Sexual Abuse** • Session 26 **Sexual Harassment and Acquaintance Rape**

UNIT ELEVEN **Celebration and Closure** 83

Principle Cards 84

United Church of Christ Religious Supplement to

Our Whole Lives Sexuality Education for Grades 7-9

Introduction to the United Church of Christ Companion 93
Opening Worship for Each Unit and Session 101
Worship Service for the Beginning of the Curriculum 103

UNIT ONE **Group Building and Examining Values** 107

Session 1 **Introduction to the Program** • Session 2 **Examining Values** •
Unit One Closing Worship

UNIT TWO **Sexuality and Body Awareness** 115

Session 3 **Sexual Language** • Session 4 **Anatomy and Physiology** •
Session 5 **Personal Concerns About Puberty** • **Unit Two Closing Worship**

UNIT THREE **Gender and Diversity** 123

Session 6 **Understanding Gender Roles** • Session 7 **Disability and Other Diversity Issues** • **Unit Three Closing Worship**

UNITS FOUR Through SEVEN 129

UNIT FOUR **Sexual Orientation and Gender Identity** 131

Session 8 **Sexual Orientation** • Session 9 **Guest Panel** • Session 10 **Gender Identity**

UNIT FIVE **Relationships** 139

Session 11 **Introduction to Relationships** • Session 12 **Relationship Skills** • Session 13 **Thorny Issues in Friendship** • Session 14 **Dating and Lifetime Commitments**

UNIT SIX **Lovemaking** 147

Session 15 **Lovemaking Is More Than Sex** • Session 16 **Masturbation and Other Sexual Behaviors**

UNIT SEVEN **Preparing for Parenthood** 151

Session 17 **Conception, Pregnancy, and Birth** • Session 18 **Teenage Pregnancy** • **Units Four Through Seven Closing Worship**

UNITS EIGHT Through TEN 157

UNIT EIGHT **Responsible Sexual Behavior** 159

Session 19 **Defining/Redefining Abstinence** • Session 20 **Contraception** • Session 21 **Unintended Pregnancy Options** • Session 22 **Sexual Decisions**

UNIT NINE **Sexually Transmitted Diseases (STDs)** 167

Session 23 **STD Facts** • Session 24 **STD Prevention**

UNIT TEN **Abuse of Sexuality** 171

Session 25 **Recovering from Sexual Abuse** • Session 26 **Sexual Harassment and Acquaintance Rape** • **Units Eight Through Ten Closing Worship**

UNIT ELEVEN **Conclusion** 181

Session 27 **Celebration and Closure**

Supporting Sexuality Education in Your Congregation

Rev. Lena Breen

Introducing sexuality education into your congregation can be a wonderful opportunity to put faith into action. It can provide a forum for members to talk about their sexual values and how these values can and do influence our society within the context of community. It can show members that sexuality education contributes to an objective held dear by virtually all people of faith: respect and justice for all, deserving of all. It can offer your congregation the opportunity to articulate and live these ideals, making it a richer source of life, hope, and support.

To offer sexuality education in a congregation is to acknowledge that human sexuality is simply too important, too beautiful, and too potentially dangerous to be ignored in a religious community. Sexuality education gives families and individuals of all ages the benefit of community support as they wrestle with sexuality issues and decisions. Although our society is saturated with images of sex, those images are often lacking in love and mutual respect. The education, worship, group activities, and advocacy encompassed in sexuality education can offer our children and youth a vision more consonant with our beliefs and values, and enhance intergenerational bonding and trust.

Yet, even in a congregation of like-minded people, sexuality education can be controversial. The subject is loaded with personal opinion and sometimes with fear and misunderstanding. Exploring sexuality education's programmatic possibilities requires hard work, courage, and an active commitment.

Effectively developing a congregational commitment, therefore, involves a four-part process of building allies, forming an oversight committee, educating and inspiring the congregation, and making the program an ongoing part of the congregation's ministry. If this work is not done, frustrations and misconceptions can develop, leading to controversy and division that can undermine or prevent the program's success.

BUILDING ALLIES

Building allies is the first step. Before attempting to institute a sexuality education program in your congregation, you will need the support of your congregation's ministers and lay leaders, such as the board of trustees, the religious education committee, the social action committee, and the youth committee. The support of individuals in the congregation who have a professional background in sexuality education or a related field, such as reproductive medicine or sex therapy, can also be valuable when representing the program to the congregation.

How can you gain this support? Learn about the history of sexuality education in your denomination and in your congregation, then explain your objectives for the program you'd like to offer. Give church leaders the opportunity to review the materials in the program, to meet with the curriculum teachers (if they have been selected), and to ask questions of the people most familiar with the program's content and values. If support doesn't come immediately, don't panic. Instead, work to continue the conversation, to discuss issues, to answer questions, and to meet individuals where they are. Expect to be an advocate for the sexuality education you believe in.

CREATING OVERSIGHT

Forming an oversight committee is the second step in building congregational support. Having committee members share the work of introducing and maintaining a program will not only make each person's workload lighter, but the input from various age and interest groups in the church will give many people a sense of ownership in the program. Their shared learning and wisdom will contribute to its success. Potential committee members include your congregation's director of religious education, parents, youth, professionals in fields related to sexuality, and representatives from other relevant groups within the church. In particular, seek to include members active in your congregation's social action committee; it is important that the religious education group is not alone in leading the effort to implement sexuality education.

What will the oversight committee do? Early on, this committee can help institute the program: creating a budget for program materials and teacher training, choosing the best resources and facilitators, coordinating sexuality education efforts with other congregational programming, and conducting activities to build support. The committee can work with the program's teachers to organize parent orientation sessions and obtain written permission from parents of all participants under the age of 18. Later, the committee can maintain the program, evaluate it regularly, and interpret the progress of the program to the congregation.

EDUCATING AND INSPIRING

The third step in developing a congregational commitment to sexuality education involves educating and inspiring parents, potential participants, and the congregation as a whole. Part of this effort might involve encouraging the congregation to think about religion and sexuality by leading worship services, sponsoring discussion groups, or developing reading lists on the subject. Survey your congregation about their interest in sexuality education and how sexuality relates to their theological and spiritual understandings. Explore whether your denomination has policy statements that an adult study group can read and discuss. Turn to your denomination's social justice department, religious education committee, or public policy office for resources that can support your efforts. The theological implications of sexuality, biblical references to sexuality, the responses of different world religions to sexuality, and issues of sexuality and justice can all be challenging and productive topics.

You will also need to educate the congregation about sexuality education and the specific curriculum you are using. Hold forums that are open to the congregation, or offer presentations about the program at congregational meetings. Announce the program in the congregation's newsletter and in Sunday bulletins. Display information on the religious education bulletin board. Provide more detailed handouts about the curriculum, the positive effects of comprehensive sexuality education, and the value of providing sexuality education in an environment centered on faith-based values. Consider joint programming for parents and youth, or courses especially for parents on communicating with their children about sexuality.

Your committee must not only educate, but also inspire. Sermons by the minister, by members of the congregation, or by youth can convey the importance and excitement that lies behind this effort. It is important to frame the issue of implementing comprehensive sexuality education in a broader context. When the congregation performs a child dedication or baptism, it commits to nurturing, loving, and educating that child. Sexuality education is part of that commitment we make to our families and our young people. It is part of the support we offer to families and children.

ONCE EDUCATION IS ESTABLISHED

The final step in starting a sexuality education program is institutionalizing it—making it part of the congregation's annual commitment to religious education. Institutionalization includes continuing administration of the curriculum by the oversight committee. The committee must also support the program teachers, by ensuring that they have proper training and by conducting background checks on new teachers. Finally, the committee should evaluate the program regularly, seek new or supplemental resources if needed, and ensure that the program continues to meet the congregation's needs effectively.

As sexuality education continues, so must advocacy. Each group of new parents, youth, teachers, and congregation members needs information about sexuality education and its connection to ministry. In addition, you may feel called to expand your congregation's advocacy into work across congregational or religious lines. Open up your sexuality education program to members of other congregations. Organize a workday at a center or local AIDS organization. Raise funds to benefit organizations that provide sexuality education. Collaborate with other organizations, religious or secular, to support comprehensive sexuality education in the community.

A major objective throughout this process is to increase communication between church members of all ages. Intergenerational communication is a valuable asset to any church. How rare are such opportunities in our society! By promoting sexuality education within your congregation, you can create opportunities to bridge these generational boundaries and to show that faith can shed light on the complicated issues of our times.

The Reverend Lena Breen served as director of the department of religious education for the Unitaran Universalist Association and cochair of the Sexuality Education Task Force of the Unitarian Universalist Association and the United Church Board for Homeland Ministries from 1998 to 2001.

Sexuality and Our Faith

A Companion to

Our Whole Lives

Grades 7–9

Unitarian Universalist

Sexuality and Our Faith

A Companion to Our Whole Lives

Grades 7–9

Reverend Makanah Elizabeth Morriss
Reverend Jory Agate

Unitarian Universalists can contact the following offices for updated lists of resources related to the *Our Whole Lives/Sexuality and Our Faith* programs in UU congregations:

Office of Bisexual, Gay, Lesbian and Transgender Concerns
Unitarian Universalist Association
25 Beacon Street
Boston, MA 02108
617/742-2100 ext. 470
http://www.uua.org/obgltc

Youth Office
Lifespan Faith Development
Unitarian Universalist Association
25 Beacon Street
Boston, MA 02108
617/742-2100 ext. 355
http://www.uua.org/yruu

Family Network
Unitarian Universalist Association
25 Beacon Street
Boston, MA 02108
617/742-2100 ext. 362
http://www.uua.org/families

Introduction to the Unitarian Universalist Companion

This supplement offers you, as religious educators and teachers, a Unitarian Universalist religious connection and foundation for *Our Whole Lives: Sexuality Education for Grades 7–9.*

What is religious about sexuality education? In liberal religious education, we seek to provide roots and wings for our children and youth. We offer them roots in our Unitarian Universalist religious traditions and values. We want our young people to be grounded in the knowledge that in our religious communities they are accepted and loved for who they are. We want them to feel good about their bodies and about being who they are in the world.

We also want to give our children and youth wings: the freedom to make meaning of their own lives; the opportunity to clarify their own values and apply them to their own experiences; the strength to develop into their own true, best selves. We want our young people to grow in integrity to respect themselves, to treat others fairly, to fight against exploitation, and to work for equality. We want to offer them wings of transformation as they seek justice for themselves and others.

As religious educators, we offer knowledge and skills in an accepting and affirming community. We offer our youth models for living out their Unitarian Universalist values, experiencing a prophetic Unitarian Universalist vision, and finding their own roles in it. We want to empower young people so that they can take care of themselves as they live out their values.

UNITARIAN UNIVERSALIST PRINCIPLES

Why do we offer sexuality education in our religious communities? We do this because of our Unitarian Universalist Principles. Four of these in particular clearly call us to offer such programs:

- **The inherent worth and dignity of every person.** We want our young people to respect the worth and dignity of their own selves, including their bodies. We want them to respect the worth and dignity of others, including those who may be different from them.

- **Justice, equity, and compassion in human relations.** *Our Whole Lives* addresses the elements of loving, equitable, and healthy relationships and counters injustices such as homophobia, stereotyping, and sexism.
- **A free and responsible search for truth and meaning.** *Our Whole Lives* invites youth to engage their minds and listen to their hearts in identifying their values and acquiring the knowledge and skills to live by them. It nurtures a trusting, respectful community in which all voices are heard.
- **The goal of world community with peace, liberty, and justice for all.** *Our Whole Lives* encourages youth to value themselves, seek healthy relationships with others, and act on their values throughout their lives.

The activities in *Our Whole Lives* connect at many points and in many ways with UU principles. Our Unitarian Universalist heritage of affirmation of the individual and courageous justice seeking are the foundations on which this program is built.

The Larger Context

The world around us offers a multitude of reasons why we need to offer comprehensive and compassionate sexuality education to our youth. Every day, the media is full of stories and images relating to sexuality. Many of these images are violent and exploitative. The "Religious Right" is very vocal in defining sexuality and "family values." Every day, expressions of fear and hostility are directed against people who are "different." All of these expressions threaten violence to the spirit or body; some end in the ultimate violence of death. We must face our community with truth, knowledge, courage, and an invitation to deeper understanding and dialogue.

As we equip our youth to lead sexually healthy and responsible lives, we help to transform a cultural climate of fear and confusion into a new reality of lives lived congruent with the values of the inherent worth and dignity of each and every person. As we invite our young people into a clearer understanding and celebration of their wholeness of being, we offer a blessing to the generations to come.

SEXUALITY EDUCATION AS RELIGIOUS EDUCATION

So, what is religious about *Our Whole Lives*? We believe that *Our Whole Lives* is religious because it seeks to nurture:

- religious community
- spiritual depth
- prophetic vision and action for justice
- values congruent with participants' religious beliefs and the skills, attitudes, and knowledge to live out those values
- the worth and dignity of every participant

Religious Community

Each *Our Whole Lives* session begins with a time of gathering and ends with a time for reflection and closure. These rituals create and nurture a sense of community. The religious dimension of that community can be deepened by creating Unitarian Universalist rituals appropriate for your group. Consider using a chalice in the gathering as the day's reading is shared. This can be a simple and yet profound way to frame for the group that they are in religious community. Use a moment of silence to deepen the sense of community. Ask the youth to help create a sacred space. Select, or have participants bring in, special objects to build a centering/focus area. This may be a low table or a cloth or small carpet on the floor. Your group may enjoy creating a centering cloth using, for example, fabric crayons or paints. Create a ritual for lighting the chalice each week. Use the Unitarian Universalist Principle cards included in this supplement by choosing those that best apply to each session, reading them, and placing them in the centering area. These are all ways to enhance the sense that this learning is occurring within religious community.

Spiritual Depth

At various points in the curriculum, we suggest ways in which you can encourage the participants' sense of spiritual depth or connection. This can occur during the rituals you use, the silences you create, or the special words or readings you share. When lights are dimmed and soft music is played, youth can often experience a deep sense of connection with the group and with their sense of a greater power beyond. It can also occur as you share with the group how this program touches *your* spiritual depth and *your* religious journey. Encourage participants to share this way, too.

Prophetic Vision and Action for Justice

As one of our hymns says so well, "We are a justice-seeking people...." *Our Whole Lives* invites awareness of issues that call for prophetic vision and action. We want our youth to realize that treating people unfairly because of their gender, body shape, physical ability, or sexual orientation is not acceptable. We want them to understand that our circle includes all brothers and sisters in our global village. We want our young people to accept others from all racial and cultural backgrounds and those with different values and perspectives.

Each group member will bring his or her own perspective to issues related to sexuality. This program calls on participants to share their understandings and feelings, to clarify their sense of equity and compassion, and to listen respectfully to each other's views to the end that new doors of understanding and action will be opened.

Adolescence is a time when young people's ability to empathize with others and to envision how to create a better world is just beginning to blossom. This is an opportune time to offer information and skills that enhance such empathy and nurture such vision. Youth may, for example, be inspired to help begin a gay/lesbian/bisexual/transgender support group or bisexual/gay/lesbian/transgender-straight alliance in their school or community, volunteer for an AIDS hospice program, or march to stop violence against women. This religious supplement offers connections with our Unitarian Universalist heritage, which calls us to prophetic vision and action and helps us draw courage for living out our values.

Clarifying Values Congruent With One's Religious Beliefs

In every session, take opportunities to ask participants to reflect on how their own religious values and beliefs connect with what they are learning about sexuality. Living our lives congruent with our values is never easy, but when we succeed, we are rewarded with a sense of centeredness, peace, and health. Our young people need to learn to identify sexuality issues in their lives, make decisions, and take actions that are healthy and responsible. Pause and ask:

- How do you as a Unitarian Universalist respond to this issue?
- How does our congregation currently respond to this issue?
- How would you *like* our congregation to respond?

The Worth and Dignity of Each Participant

Perhaps the most religious aspect of this curriculum, and the cornerstone upon which it is built, is the belief in the worth and dignity of each participant. You, as educator, model this belief in the respectful and caring way you interact with participants and invite them to interact with each other. In creating an accepting and affirming atmosphere in the program, you will build a trusting and caring community in which each individual feels accepted, respected, and affirmed for her or his true self. Providing this experience is truly a gift of religious community.

THE LEADERS' ROLE

This supplement offers many suggestions to help youth make Unitarian Universalist connections—connections with our principles, connections with our liberal religious heritage, connections with their own evolving sense of religious values and religious identity.

We invite *you*, as leaders, to be aware of how leading this program strengthens *your* Unitarian Universalist connections and enhances *your* religious journey. Your modeling of such an awareness is probably the most effective teaching technique. As you explore and understand the relationship between session topics and your sense of Unitarian Universalism, you will find your youth doing the same.

USING THIS RESOURCE

This supplement includes ideas for each unit and specific suggestions for each session to make connections with Unitarian Universalism. Specific enrichment ideas are described under the appropriate session number and name of activity in the core curriculum, *Our Whole Lives: Sexuality Education for Grades 7-9.*

We suggest that you read the *Our Whole Lives* session plan first and then turn to this companion resource for ideas on how to enhance the program with Unitarian Universalist perspectives and values.

Important Notes About the Slide Illustrations

This religious education companion to *Our Whole Lives* contains instructions for the use of a set of black-and-white, hand-drawn slides illustrating three topics: anatomy, masturbation, and lovemaking. The following are important points to know about these visuals:

- The use of the slides is optional. You can offer comprehensive sexuality education and a rich religious education experience without them.
- The slides can be purchased only by UU and UCC congregations that have *Our Whole Lives*-trained teachers and are for use only within the congregation's religious education program.
- A script and special parent orientation accompany the set of slides.
- **Use of the slides requires a special parent/guardian permission form.** The permission form in the *Our Whole Lives* curriculum is not adequate as it does not mention the slides. The appropriate permission form follows this Introduction.
- If you plan to show the slides to youth, you must give parents the opportunity to view them in the context of a Parent Orientation session. Parents have a right to view these and any other curricular materials their children will experience.
- Since each slide presentation requires time not scheduled in the core curriculum, you will need to adapt your schedule to accommodate them. Modifications may include dropping an activity in the *Our Whole Lives* curriculum, extending the session time, or scheduling extra sessions.

IN CONCLUSION

We welcome you to the journey that you and your group are about to begin with *Our Whole Lives.* It is our hope that your religious and spiritual connection will be strengthened as you help your group experience connections between their religion and their sexuality for their whole lives.

Permission Form

I/We give ____
child(ren)'s name(s)

permission to participate in *Our Whole Lives: Sexuality Education for Grades 7–9*, part of the

education program at ____
(name of organization)

I/We understand that the program includes use of explicit visual materials.
I/We have viewed, or declined the opportunity to view, these materials.
I/We have attended an orientation to this program.

Signed ______________________
(parent/guardian)

Name ______________________
(print)

Address ______________________

____

____

Phone Number

Daytime ______________________

Evening ______________________

Date signed ______________________

Signed ______________________
(parent/guardian)

Name ______________________
(print)

Address ______________________

____

____

Phone Number

Daytime ______________________

Evening ______________________

Date signed ______________________

Group Building and Examining Values

The two sessions of Unit One offer an orientation to the program, begin the process of building group trust and a sense of religious community, and lay the foundation for participants to examine their values and the relationship of those values to behavior. In this unit, you will also introduce the Unitarian Universalist Principles, which you will reference throughout the program. The Principles can serve to anchor *Our Whole Lives* in our religious traditions, beliefs, and values.

In Session One and throughout the program, take advantage of group-building activities such as games and opening and closing rituals. Even if most participants are already familiar with each other, it is important to create a cohesive, trusting group at *this* time around *this* topic. Game resources are listed in the resource section of *Our Whole Lives*, and a catolog of Young Religious Unitarian Universalists (YRUU) resources can be obtained from the Unitarian Universalist Association (UUA) Youth Office (617/742-2100 or E-mail: yruu@uua.org).

To strengthen the experience of religious community in this program, we suggest you give some thought to the opening ritual you will use throughout the program. The ritual could include any or all of the following:

- Bring in a chalice to light during the opening and closing rituals of every session.
- Create a centering/focus area on a low table or on a piece of carpet on the floor.
- Cover the centering/focus area with a cloth you bring in or have participants decorate a plain cloth with their names and a symbol of themselves. Fabric paint, fabric crayons, or permanent markers can be easily used for this activity.
- From time to time, bring in, or invite participants to bring in, appropriate symbolic objects to place on the centering/focus table. You can vary the objects depending on the session theme, or you can display the same symbols throughout the program.
- Use a meditation gong or chimes to introduce a moment of silence.

- Use soft, meditative music for a time of reflection. Leaders and participants can take turns bringing in selections.
- Photocopy the Unitarian Universalist Principle graphics (at the end of this section) onto heavy paper. When folded in half, these make stand-up Unitarian Universalist Principle cards to place on the centering/focus table. One or more can be placed on the table each session to emphasize the connection between sexuality and Unitarian Universalist values and beliefs.
- Hang a poster of the UUA Principles and Sources in the meeting space throughout the program.

Introduction to the Program

PREPARATION (page 2)

Add:

- Have markers, index cards, and other materials for participants to decorate the Question Box as they arrive.

WELCOME AND INTRODUCTIONS (page 3)

In addition to the suggestions in the curriculum, emphasize that *Our Whole Lives* gives participants a place where their points of view will be listened to and valued by all in the group, both leaders and youth.

WARM-UP ACTIVITIES

Do not minimize the importance of the Warm-Up Activities and other group-building exercises. These are some of the most important parts of each session.

As you introduce the games, share with the youth that having time to "hang out" and socialize with peers is something that Unitarian Universalists value. Through games, we get to know each other in different ways. The group will build its own connections. Creating a history of "fun times" is one of the best ways to create a group identity.

GROUP COVENANT (page 6)

When you list the ground rules, be sure to say something like the following: "What is said in this room will stay in this room unless we feel that you or someone else has been hurt or is in danger of being hurt. If we feel that is the case, we will talk with you privately before we decide on any other action."

Before beginning this program, check with your minister(s) and religious educator to determine the policies in your congregation related to confidentiality and the policies and procedures related to reporting abuse.

PROGRAM RITUALS

R&R (page 7)

Lighting the chalice is a good way to begin this time of reconnection as a group. This is the time to introduce the opening ritual you have planned. (See Additional Preparation for suggestions.)

Question Box (page 8)

To add a sense of Unitarian Universalist community, invite each participant to make a question mark (you might hand out half of an index card to each participant) to put on the question box. The Question Box can be placed on the centering/focus table.

Examining Values

As the participants work on examining values, it is important to help them clarify and articulate their individual UU values. At various points throughout the session, invite reflection on the relationship between their values and what they have learned about Unitarian Universalist values from their parents, their religious education program, and other experiences of congregational life.

As the youth share their values, emphasize that, as Unitarian Universalists, we embrace a diversity of beliefs. We do not have to agree with someone else's values, but we should be careful not to put any person down because of the values or beliefs he or she expresses. This is often difficult for youth, especially if they hear their parents and other adults being less than tolerant. Nevertheless, if participants can clearly and positively articulate their values and beliefs in this group and can listen respectfully to others, they will be living our Unitarian Universalist Principles in transformative ways for those around them. It is an ambitious goal but one well worth pursuing. This session offers lots of practice.

R&R (page 17)

Opening Ritual

Before participants arrive, have the centering area set up with the chalice, the Question Box, and the special cloth or symbolic objects you have chosen. Begin by lighting the chalice. You may want to introduce a moment of silent centering using a meditation chime or gong. Whatever opening you design, beginning each session with the same simple ritual helps participants connect with each other and helps anchor your group in religious community.

IDENTIFYING PERSONAL VALUES (page 20)

3. Add to the list of posted questions:
   - Which of these are Unitarian Universalist values? Is there a UU Principle that indicates to you that this is a value?

REFLECTION AND PLANNING FOR NEXT SESSION

Closing Ritual: Try using a chime or bell for a moment of silence.

Sexuality and Body Awareness

This unit focuses on understanding, accepting, and affirming our physical bodies with all their beauty and uniqueness. One of the Unitarian Universalist Principles we affirm is "a free and responsible search for truth and meaning." In this unit, the search for truth includes the most up-to-date information on the sexual aspects of our bodies.

Youth may find the topic difficult to talk about. We invite you to model acceptance of and comfort with the human body. As you affirm the inherent beauty of all bodies, no matter what their age or shape, you will offer our youth a powerful message. As you share information about how bodies change shape and responsiveness over a lifetime, you will offer participants healthy acceptance of the gifts of each age.

As Unitarian Universalists, we value the gift of life, which is manifested in our bodies. We believe that the human body is inherently good, not sinful, and that we are called to care for and respect our bodies. The pleasures of the senses are not temptations but ways in which we can experience and be grateful for the wonders of life. We know that any gift can be misused or abused, and our commitment is to honor and respect the human body, our own as well as others'.

Sexual Language

R&R (page 26)

Opening Ritual

Before participants arrive, have the centering/focus area set up with the chalice, the Question Box, and the special cloth or symbolic objects you have chosen. Begin by lighting the chalice. You may want to introduce a moment of silent centering using a meditation chime or gong. Beginning each session with the same simple ritual helps participants connect with each other and helps anchor your group in its religious identity.

BREAKING THE LANGUAGE BARRIER (page 27)

6. Add to the discussion questions:

- Are there any words or terms that we want to covenant not to use in this group?
- Are there any words or terms that seem to go against our Unitarian Universalist values because they are used as put-downs?

SEXUALITY IS EVERYWHERE COLLAGE (page 28)

4. Add the following to the discussion questions:

- How are our Unitarian Universalist values about sexuality represented in the images in your collages? How are our Unitarian Universalist values *not* represented?

Anatomy and Physiology

Again, we want to share with youth our Unitarian Universalist value that our bodies are sacred and to be respected. This session helps participants learn that our whole bodies are sexual and can offer the gifts of pleasure.

In this session, we focus on the Unitarian Universalist search for truth by offering students a fun way to obtain accurate information about their sexuality. As Unitarian Universalists, we value obtaining accurate information about our bodies and our sexuality.

If you choose to use the slide visuals, have available the set of anatomy drawings developed for this session. We suggest you show these slides after the Constructing Sexual Systems activity. Of course, you will need to adjust your meeting time or your session plan if you include this activity. Preview the slides and read the script and discussion questions. Be sure the projection equipment is in good operating condition for the session.

R&R (page 37)

Opening Ritual

Before participants arrive, have the centering/focus area set up with the chalice, the Question Box, and the special cloth or symbolic objects you have chosen. Begin by lighting the chalice. You may want to introduce a moment of silent centering using a meditation chime or gong. You may also want to place on the table the Unitarian Universalist Principle card, "We affirm and promote the free and responsible search for truth." Beginning each session with the same simple ritual helps students connect with each other and helps anchor your group in its religious identity.

CONSTRUCTING SEXUAL SYSTEMS (page 38)

6. Add to the discussion questions:

- Do you think our search for truth as Unitarian Universalists should include gaining accurate, up-to-date information about human sexuality? Why or why not?

ANATOMY SLIDES

Show the anatomy slides using the script and discussion questions that accompany the slide set.

REFLECTION AND PLANNING FOR NEXT SESSION (page 39)

3. Say, "As Unitarian Universalists, we believe it is important that truth and knowledge is shared and passed on to others."

Personal Concerns About Puberty

This session provides an opportunity to emphasize the affirmation of the inherent worth and dignity of every person, no matter what their age or size or shape. Participants' personal concerns about puberty will likely focus on body image. Unitarian Universalism encourages acceptance of one another for who we are, not what we look like. We value diversity, not uniformity. Throughout the session, emphasize this perspective directly and indirectly. Focus on the value of each individual and the particular gifts and talents each has to offer the world. Who is smaller or bigger does not need to be the concern. People come in all sizes and shapes. People mature at different rates. What matters is that we treat ourselves and others with kindness and respect. Your ability to listen empathetically to students' questions and concerns and your reassurance about their physical development and sense of self will model for them the kind of acceptance and affirmation they need for a healthy attitude toward the human body and sexuality.

R&R (page 43)

Opening Ritual

Set up your centering/focus area before participants arrive. You may want to place the Unitarian Universalist Principle card, "We affirm and promote the inherent worth and dignity of every person," near the chalice. Begin with your opening ritual of chalice lighting, silence, and the other aspects your group has chosen.

AM I NORMAL? (page 45)

5. Add to the discussion questions:

- In Unitarian Universalist congregations, we talk about inherent worth and dignity. What does that mean to you when you think of body image?

REFLECTION AND PLANNING FOR THE NEXT SESSION (page 47)

1. Add:

- As a Unitarian Universalist, I believe each person's body is…

Gender and Diversity

This unit focuses on two equity issues: gender roles and the exclusion or stereotyping of people with disabilities. These topics relate directly to our Principles, which affirm "justice, equity, and compassion in human relations" and "the inherent worth and dignity of every person."

Session Six focuses on gender. Our tradition honors gender equity, a value evident in our worship themes, music, and religious education curricula; in the stand that our people have historically taken for rights for women; and in the many resolutions passed by our annual General Assembly.

Our long and valued tradition includes women and men who have acted courageously on behalf of equity for both men and women and for justice and compassion for those with disabilities. You may want to mention some of these leaders—for example, Susan B. Anthony and Dorothea Dix—with whom participants may be familiar. Unitarian Universalists believe that different people have different strengths and abilities. However, we believe that no one should be denied respect or opportunity on the basis of gender or ability.

Understanding Gender Roles

> We hold these truths to be self-evident; that all men and women are created equal.
>
> —From "Declaration of Sentiments and Resolutions," The First Woman's Rights Convention (1848)

> Men their rights and nothing more; women their rights and nothing less.
>
> —SUSAN B. ANTHONY and ELIZABETH CADY STANTON, motto of the newspaper, *Revolution* (1868)

Unitarians and Universalists have a strong and proud history of supporting gender equity. Susan B. Anthony was a woman from our religious history who worked with courage and commitment for this cause. Although often subjected to verbal abuse and physical threats, she persevered.

Unitarians and Universalists were among the earliest to ordain women to the ministry. The Transcendentalist movement, founded by Ralph Waldo Emerson and Henry David Thoreau, had in its midst some of the most brilliant minds of the mid-eighteenth century, including Margaret Fuller.

It is especially important in this session to help participants understand that gender equity is a foundation block of our liberal tradition. You may want to share the above quotes and information with the group. It is important to share with participants that our Unitarian Universalist Principles call us to value each gender and treat everyone with fairness.

R&R (page 59)

Opening Ritual

Prepare the centering/focus area before participants arrive. You may want to use the Unitarian Universalist Principle card, "We affirm and promote the inherent worth and dignity of every person." Begin with the opening ritual that you and your group have developed.

As you light your chalice for this session, you might want to invite the group to sing (or read the words to) Hymn #23, "Bring Many Names," in *Singing the Living Tradition*. This hymn honors both male and female images of the energy of the Creative Source of our universe. After the hymn, ask participants how each of the images felt to them as they sang the words.

Reading (page 59)

3. Following the Sojourner Truth reading add:

- For Sojourner Truth, God was male. Do Unitarian Universalists believe that God is male? Have you heard words in hymns or readings in our services that refer to God as "she" or "mother" instead of or in addition to "he" or "father"? What do you think of this?

GENDER ROLES VALUES VOTING (page 61)

3. Add to the Values Voting Statements:

- Unitarian Universalists believe that all people are equal. Do you agree?
- Unitarian Universalists believe in gender equity. Agree or disagree: Gender equity means everything for men and women should be the same.

6. Add to the discussion questions:

- How do you think your congregation lives up to its value of gender equity? (For example, is there a baby-changing table in both the women's and men's restrooms?)

IN THE BOX

***Part One:* Brainstorming** (page 63)

9. Add the following points:

- As Unitarian Universalists, we believe in the inherent worth and dignity of all people, and respect all persons whether or not they conform to the current box for their gender.
- As Unitarian Universalists, we believe that men and women should have equal opportunities and should not be stereotyped.

REFLECTION AND PLANNING FOR THE NEXT SESSION (page 66)

2. Add to optional homework assignments:

- Take a good look at our congregation. What gender-role stereotypes do you see? Talk with your minister or religious educator about actions that can be taken to encourage gender equity in our congregations. Then take those actions!

Disability and Other Diversity Issues

One goal of this session is to empower young people to act compassionately with those who may be different from them. This takes courage. Courage is nurtured by deeply rooted values and convictions. Unitarian Universalist values are a good source for such courage. Many women and men in our past and in the present have quietly and courageously helped transform the actions of their local neighborhoods and communities. The youth you teach today will be those citizens of tomorrow.

R&R (page 70)

Opening Ritual

Set up centering/focus area before participants arrive. You may want to use the Unitarian Universalist Principle cards affirming inherent worth and dignity and justice, equity, and compassion in human relations. If your congregation has an accessibilities committee or task force, include something symbolizing the work of that group.

Reading

3. Add to discussion questions:

- Would Ofelia be able to participate fully in your congregation? What would need to be changed to make this possible?

WHAT WOULD YOU DO? (page 71)

3. Add the following point:

- As Unitarian Universalists, we value every individual no matter her or his ability, race, sexual orientation, or gender, and we believe all individuals should be able to find a welcoming religious home in our congregations.

4. Add the following question:

- What do you think your congregation can do to become more welcoming of each individual who wishes to come here?

OPTIONAL ACTIVITIES (page 74)

If you present the four stages of relating to differences, add the questions:

- Where do you think your congregation falls in these stages?
- How important is it to you to belong to a congregation that is a bridge builder in these ways?
- What is one step your group could take to help increase your congregation's awareness of these issues?

Sexual Orientation and Gender Identity

The first two sessions of Unit Four help participants explore the topic of sexual orientation. The third session addresses the equally challenging topic of diversity in gender identity.

Unitarian Universalists have been at the forefront of religious institutions willing to affirm and support diversity of sexual orientation. Our annual General Assembly (GA) has provided a continental platform for our Unitarian Universalist voice to be heard on this important issue.

In 1970, a general resolution was passed at General Assembly calling upon all Unitarian Universalists to stand together to "end discrimination against homosexuals and bisexuals." The following year, the Reverend Richard Nash and Elgin Blair cofounded the Gay Caucus to lobby for an Office of Gay Affairs. In that same year, *About Your Sexuality* was published. It presented homosexuality and bisexuality from a positive perspective. In 1973, another General Resolution created the Unitarian Universalist Association (UUA) Office of Gay Affairs, to be staffed by gay people. In 1977, a General Resolution urged Unitarian Universalists to fight antigay propaganda. In 1980, a GA Business Resolution called upon the UUA to assist in the settlement of openly gay ministers. Another Business Resolution in 1984 affirmed UUA clergy who were conducting same-gender Services of Union. In 1987, a General Resolution was passed calling upon Unitarian Universalists to work to overturn antigay/lesbian/bisexual legislation. A Business Resolution passed in 1989 adopted the Welcoming Congregation program to combat homophobia. That same year, another General Resolution opposed discrimination against people with AIDS/HIV. In 1992, a Resolution of Immediate Witness opposed hate campaigns in Oregon and Colorado. The 1993 General Assembly in Charlotte, North Carolina, included a public candlelight vigil in protest of North Carolina's "crime against nature" laws. In that year, the UUA Office of Gay Affairs changed its name to the Office of Lesbian, Bisexual and Gay Concerns. The UUA also publicly endorsed the March on Washington for Lesbian, Gay, and Bisexual Equal Rights. In 1994, a Resolution of Immediate Witness was passed and urged that sexuality education in public schools be inclusive of all sexual orientations. In 1996, the UUA Board of Trustees passed a resolution in support of same-gender marriage, and the UUA Office of Lesbian, Bisexual, and Gay Concerns became the

Office of Bisexual, Gay, Lesbian, and Transgender Concerns. (For more information about UUA support of B/G/L/T issues, contact that office at the UUA: 617/742-2100.)

In addition, Young Religious Unitarian Universalists (YRUU) has been active in affirming and welcoming gay, lesbian, bisexual, and transgender youth. In pamphlets developed by the YRUU Youth Program Specialists, in various resolutions passed at YRUU's annual Youth Council, and in the atmosphere of caring and acceptance found in local YRUU youth groups across the continent, the message is the same. We, as Unitarian Universalists, live out our belief in the inherent worth and dignity of all people and our support of justice, equity, and compassion in human relations in the way we welcome people of all sexual orientations and stand for equal rights for all.

It is important for you and your participants to be aware of this history. We encourage you to contact the UUA Bookstore to order copies of the most current welcoming pamphlet for lesbian, bisexual, gay, and transgender people so that you can share them with your group. We can be proud of our history, which will provide affirmation and comfort for some youth in your group who may be certain of, or may be wondering about, their own sexual orientations.

For the guest panel suggested in Session Nine, it can be very valuable to have members of your own congregation speak to your group. Youth can benefit from talking with someone they know and can speak to in the future if they have further questions and concerns. It is important for youth, especially gay, lesbian, bisexual, and transgender youth, to have adults they can look up to as role models and mentors. Thus, this guest panel can be an invaluable contribution your congregation can offer the youth.

A caution, however. If you invite guest panelists from your congregation, be sure that they are very comfortable with being out, and that they are comfortable talking with young people of this age. Your help and support as they take on this new task will be very important. If you are unable to use speakers from your own congregation, consider inviting speakers from a neighboring Unitarian Universalist congregation.

One of the primary goals of religious education is to enable and empower people of all ages not only to clarify and understand their religious values, but also to live them. Session Ten focuses on challenging sexual identity issues in society and invites participants to reflect on individual and group actions that might be helpful and appropriate now and throughout their lives.

As Unitarian Universalists, we commit ourselves to justice, equity, and compassion for all, regardless of sexual orientation or gender identity. Our belief in the inherent worth and dignity of every person requires us to act on our values.

Be aware of actions your congregation is taking either as a whole or in small groups or committees that address the issues raised in this unit. Share with your group any information you have about these activities including pictures and schedules of events.

Sexual Orientation

MATERIALS CHECKLIST (page 80)

- Obtain from the UUA Bookstore copies for all participants of the most recent welcoming pamphlet for lesbian, bisexual, gay, and transgender people.
- Ask your minister or religious educator to borrow Unitarian Universalist T-shirts and buttons with welcoming messages regarding sexual orientation.

R&R (page 82)

Opening Ritual

Prepare the centering/focus area before participants arrive. You may want to include one of the BGLT welcoming pamphlets and/or UU T-shirts and buttons with welcoming messages regarding sexual orientation. You also may want to place near the chalice the Unitarian Universalist Principle cards affirming the inherent worth and dignity of every person and justice, equity, and compassion in human relations.

LECTURETTE: BELIEFS ABOUT SEXUAL ORIENTATION AND HOMOPHOBIA (page 84)

1. Add to the introduction:

> Hand out YRUU welcoming pamphlets to participants. Share with the group that since 1970, the UUA has passed a series of resolutions affirming diversity of sexual orientation. Read the pamphlet with the group.

2. Add to discussion questions:

- How do you feel about our denomination's stance?

MYTHINFORMATION GAME, LEADER RESOURCE 9 (page 89)

Add the statements below to Leader Resource 9, Myth/Fact Statements and Answers. The statements relate to what can be found in the Christian Bible and Jewish scriptures about homosexuality.

17. In the Christian Bible, Jesus condemned homosexuality.

MYTH. Jesus taught that showing love toward people and meeting their needs was often more important than following the letter of the scriptural laws of his day, and in the Christian scriptures, he never mentioned either homosexuality or homosexual behavior.

18. In Jewish scriptures, homosexuals are condemned for feeling the way they do.

MYTH. The Jewish language, Hebrew, has no word for homosexuality, and we do not think that affectional orientation was well understood in biblical times. There are Jewish scriptural passages that condemn some homosexual behaviors, even as there are passages that condemn other sexual behaviors that do not lead to procreation.

VALUES VOTING, LEADER RESOURCE 12 (page 95)

Add the following to Leader Resource 12, Sexual Orientation Values Voting Statements. They are specifically related to responses to sexual orientation in your congregation.

11. I would feel very comfortable if my minister was gay, lesbian, or bisexual.

12. I think our church (fellowship) should perform marriages for lesbian, gay, and bisexual couples.

13. I would feel comfortable if my youth group advisor was lesbian, gay, or bisexual.

REFLECTION AND PLANNING FOR NEXT SESSION (page 87)

Add the following questions for discussion:

- How safe do you think our congregation is for gay, lesbian, and bisexual youth?
- What do you think we can do about it?

Guest Panel

R&R (page 100)

Opening Ritual

Set up the centering/focus area before participants arrive. As you did last session, you may want to add objects or symbols that express Unitarian Universalism's affirmation of gay, lesbian, bisexual, and transgender people. You may want to use the Unitarian Universalist Principle card affirming support of justice, equity, and compassion in human relations.

GUEST SPEAKERS (page 101)

3. If a guest speaker is a member of your congregation or another Unitarian Universalist congregation, add to discussion questions:

- How has it been for you to be a gay man/lesbian/bisexual in this congregation?

Gender Identity

The focus on the inherent worth and dignity of every person is very important in this session. Call the UUA Office of Bisexual, Gay, Lesbian, and Transgender Concerns for an information packet about transgender definitions and issues. This material will be very helpful in answering participants' questions.

R&R (page 104)

Opening Ritual

Set up centering/focus area before participants arrive. If you have any pictures of groups in your congregation who are working on the issues in this unit, include them in your centering area. Use the Unitarian Universalist Principle card affirming the inherent worth and dignity of every person and any other cards you feel are particularly relevant.

REFLECTION AND PLANNING FOR NEXT SESSION (page 107)

2. Add the following questions:
   - What Unitarian Universalist values are relevant to today's session?
   - How do Unitarian Universalist religious values help us understand and be supportive of sexual diversity in society?
   - How do you think our congregation would respond/has responded to a transgender individual? How could the congregation be supportive?

Relationships

This unit focuses on relationships and the qualities of healthy, happy relationships. Participants are invited to look honestly at issues and concerns that arise in relationships and to practice skills to handle these issues and develop good relationships.

The Unitarian Universalist Principle that is the focus of these sessions is our affirmation to promote "justice, equity, and compassion in human relations." It is important that our youth understand that, as Unitarian Universalists, we believe in the importance of living out this Principle in all of our relationships. This Principle is at the core of our sense of connection with others.

Introduction to Relationships

R&R (page 116)

Opening Ritual

Set up the centering/focus area before participants arrive. You may want to place the Unitarian Universalist Principle card "We affirm and promote justice, equity, and compassion in human relations" near the chalice. Begin with the opening ritual your group has developed.

WHAT'S IMPORTANT IN A RELATIONSHIP? (page 117)

7. Add to discussion questions:

- One reason people belong to churches is to develop friendships. How has belonging to your congregation helped you develop friendships? Are they different from school friendships?

Relationship Skills

In this session, it is important to help participants link our first Unitarian Universalist Principle, "to affirm and promote the inherent worth and dignity of every person," with their motivation to develop skills that promote respectful, compassionate, healthy relationships. Emphasize this link in each of the activities. This is a key connection for youth who are at the developmental stage in which empathy and creative altruism are activated.

LEARNING OBJECTIVES (page 122)

Add:

- To connect the practice of good listening skills with honoring the inherent worth and dignity of every person and using compassion in human relations.

R&R (page 123)

Opening Ritual

Set up the centering/focus area before participants arrive. You may want to use the Unitarian Universalist Principle card that affirms the inherent worth and dignity of every person as an object for your opening ritual.

Thorny Issues in Friendship

LEARNING OBJECTIVES (page 133)

Add:

- To identify how Unitarian Universalist principles and values can help in decision making.

R&R (page 134)

Opening Ritual

Before your group arrives, set up the centering/focus area. You may want to place the Unitarian Universalist Principle card affirming justice, equity, and compassion in human relations near the chalice.

PRESSURE IN ACTION (page 135)

8. Add to the discussion questions:

- Is the peer pressure you experience at church different from the peer pressure you experience at school? How?

DECISION MAKING: BEING CLEAR WITH YOUR FRIENDS (page 137)

2. When making a decision, add:

- Think about whether each choice goes along with your Unitarian Universalist values.

3. Add to Step 4, Consider the risks:

- Does it go against my Unitarian Universalist values?

Dating and Lifetime Commitments

This session helps participants focus on the emotional qualities needed in close relationships. We want to encourage youth to seek such qualities for themselves and to offer such qualities to others.

It is very important to help participants keep in mind how our affirmation of the "inherent worth and dignity of every person" and our commitment to promote "justice, equity, and compassion in human relations" are core values to help guide decisions and responses to dating situations.

As the session is inclusive and does not assume heterosexuality, it will be important to acknowledge that although individuals may be uncomfortable with sexual orientations other than their own, it is never acceptable to treat others with a lack of respect.

In this and every session it is important to refer to both the *Our Whole Lives* Program Values and our Unitarian Universalist Principles and Sources to help participants understand how healthy relationships and sexuality are part of our religious values.

R&R (page 144)

Opening Ritual

Set up the centering/focus area before participants arrive. You may want to use the Unitarian Universalist principles cards affirming the inherent worth and dignity of every individual and justice, equity, and compassion in human relationships. You may also want to find a picture or image that affirms these values.

YES, NO, MAYBE SO (page 145)

6. Add:

- As Unitarian Universalists, we believe in the inherent worth and dignity of all people and want to treat each other with compassion. What are ways to accept or reject offers that will still help people feel good about themselves?

Lovemaking

Unit Six focuses on an important and challenging topic—lovemaking. It is a topic about which seventh through ninth graders need full information to help them make healthy and responsible decisions. A major goal of *Our Whole Lives* is to help participants develop skills that will serve them throughout their lives. Thus, the program offers extensive information that is important not only for present but also for future decisions and experiences.

In affirming the development of a healthy sexuality, it is important to point out that experiencing sexuality with someone you care about is a wonderful, satisfying aspect of life and that there are many ways to enjoy sexual pleasure without engaging in intercourse. We want to encourage youth to wait until they are older and in a committed relationship to experience intercourse. Our society has historically offered two options for sexual intimacy—abstinence or penetration. This program offers our youth a third option, that of experiencing sensuality, intimacy, and sexual pleasure without intercourse, an option that will enhance their relationships throughout their lives. In Unit Eight: Responsible Sexual Behavior, participants will be invited to explore the third option in depth.

Unitarian Universalists affirm a "free and responsible search for truth." *Our Whole Lives* offers information in a safe and positive educational setting that affirms the goodness of human sexuality while also affirming the belief that waiting until one is older to experience sexual intercourse is a wise decision.

Lovemaking Is More Than Sex

In this session, you may choose to use the lovemaking slides that are available to congregations with *Our Whole Lives*-trained leaders. These drawings have been developed to share full information with our youth while emphasizing that the intimacy of lovemaking calls for caring and responsibility.

MATERIALS CHECKLIST (page 158)

Add:

- Lovemaking slides, slide projector, screen (optional)

PREPARATION

Add:

- Preview the slides and accompanying script to become familiar and comfortable with them.

R&R

Opening Ritual

Set up the centering/focus area before participants arrive. You may want to include the Unitarian Universalist Principle card affirming the free and responsible search for truth and meaning.

LOVEMAKING: MYTH VS. FACT (page 161)

If you are showing the lovemaking slides, drop this activity and substitute the visuals.

LOVEMAKING SLIDES

- Before showing the slides, explain to the group that a range of emotional responses to the slides is possible and acceptable. Some may experience sexual arousal; some may experience disgust; some may feel nothing; some may feel shame or interest, etc. Reassure participants that all of these reactions are normal.

- Point out that many of them have seen images of explicit sexual behavior in magazines, in movies, and on television. Many of these images are violent or exploitative, depicting abuse, coercion, and the use of sexuality to sell products. Unitarian Universalists reject teachings and behaviors that devalue or exploit human sexuality or devalue individuals or groups of people. Tell the group that the slides they are about to see show lovemaking as a positive, caring, and responsible act between mature adults. These slides were developed to give participants in this program information that may help them make clear and responsible decisions about sexual activity.
- When showing the lovemaking slides, stand near the screen, so you can speak about and point to the projected image. Modeling comfort with the sexual images offers a very important gift of acceptance to your youth. Show the slides through once without commentary. Ask for general comments or questions.
- Show the slides again, referring to the script that accompanies the slides, stopping to ask questions, answering participants' questions, and inviting comments.
- Tell the group that the slides will be available again next session if questions occur to them after this session.

Masturbation and Other Sexual Behaviors

One of the topics for this session is masturbation. One program goal is to legitimize masturbation as a healthy sexual expression. This session plan offers several different ways to talk with your group about masturbation.

As Unitarian Universalists, our reason and values call us to acknowledge the value of sexual self-love. Masturbation offers an option for safe, healthy, and developmentally appropriate sexual activity for teenagers. Throughout the lifespan, masturbation is an option available to experience pleasure and relieve sexual tension when other forms of sexual activity are unavailable or unwise. Our intent is to present the topic of masturbation in a positive context. This is not, however, an attempt to present a "how-to" of masturbation.

In this session, you may choose to show the slides on the topic of masturbation. If you plan to include them, adjust your schedule or session plan to accommodate the additional time required.

MATERIALS CHECKLIST (page 168)

Add:

- Lovemaking and masturbation slides, slide projector, screen (optional).

PREPARATION

Add:

- Preview the masturbation slides and the accompanying script to become familiar and comfortable with them.

R&R

Opening Ritual

Set up the centering/focus area before participants arrive. You may want to use the Unitarian Universalist Principle card affirming a free and responsible search for truth and meaning as well as an image symbolic of that value.

LOVEMAKING QUESTIONS AND ANSWERS (page 169)

Invite participants to write down any questions that have occurred to them during the week relating to the slides they saw last session. Following the usual Question Box procedure, have all the participants write something on a piece of paper for the box whether or not they actually have a question.

In answering these questions, you may want to revisit some of the lovemaking slides.

MASTURBATION

2. Add:

Share with the youth that as Unitarian Universalists, we believe that healthy sexual expression is important and that masturbation can be one aspect of sexual health. Include the points that masturbation offers an option for safe, healthy, and developmentally appropriate sexual activity for teenagers. Throughout life, masturbation is an option available to experience sexual pleasure and relieve sexual tension when other forms of sexual activity are unavailable or unwise. As Unitarian Universalists, our reason and values call us to acknowledge the value of sexual self-love. As Unitarian Universalists, we also value choice. Many people masturbate at some time in their lives; some never do. It is a matter of personal choice that each person can make in accordance with his or her own values and preferences.

MASTURBATION SLIDES

- Before showing the slides, explain to the group that a range of emotional responses to the slides is possible and acceptable. Some may experience sexual arousal; some may experience disgust; some may feel nothing; some may feel shame or interest, etc. Reassure participants that all of these reactions are normal.
- When showing the slides, stand near the screen, so you can speak about and point to the projected image. Modeling comfort with the sexual images offers a very important gift of acceptance to your youth. Show the slides through once without commentary. Ask for general comments or questions.
- Show the slides again, stopping to ask questions, answer participants' questions, and invite comments. As you did with the lovemaking slides, stand near the screen to talk about the images. Remember that your level of comfort with this material will convey an important message to your group.

Preparing for Parenthood

Unit Seven addresses topics that are often covered, although less completely, in health education classes in school. Within a congregational setting, the goals are to offer full information so that youth are able to make responsible decisions and to affirm our Unitarian Universalist values that the creation of a new life is a special and wondrous gift that needs to be carefully planned.

This unit can also reinforce three themes of this curriculum: experiencing sexuality with someone you care about is a wonderful, satisfying aspect of life; there are many ways to enjoy sexual pleasure without engaging in intercourse; it is important to delay bringing a new life into this world until you are in a position to care adequately for a child. Unit Seven offers youth knowledge, insights, and skills to use whenever they face situations that call for decisions about pregnancy prevention and childbearing.

Relevant Unitarian Universalist Principles include affirming the inherent worth and dignity of every person—born and unborn—so that all may have a fair start in life and justice, equity, and compassion in human relations so that the families that are created offer a just and healthy environment for their members. As Unitarian Universalists, we encourage responsible decisions related to childbearing. We also support those agencies, both public and private, that nurture and encourage parents, no matter what their ages, in the hard work of raising children.

Conception, Planned Pregnancy, and Birth

R&R (page 179)

Opening Ritual

Before participants arrive, set up the centering/focus area. You may want to bring pictures of your own children as newborns or infants or a picture of an infant at an event at your church. The Unitarian Universalist Principle card affirming the inherent worth and dignity of every person is appropriate for this session.

Teenage Pregnancy

In this session, help participants connect our Unitarian Universalist value of caring for the inherent worth and dignity of every person with the stresses of parenting. Also help them connect our value of equity and compassion in human relations with the need to provide adequate parenting and resources for the children they bring into the world.

R&R (page 189)

Opening Ritual

Set up the centering/focus area before participants arrive. You may want to include a rattle or other baby toy and the Unitarian Universalist Principle card that affirms justice, equity, and compassion in human relations.

Responsible Sexual Behavior

As Unitarian Universalists, our belief in responsible sexual behavior is firmly rooted in our first two Unitarian Universalist Principles: the inherent worth and dignity of every person and justice, equity, and compassion in human relations. These Principles apply to our decisions regarding how we want to be treated and how we want to treat others.

Being a sexual being is being a whole being. Sexuality is not just about intercourse. Healthy sexuality is about celebrating the gifts of love, intimacy, and sexual responsiveness in a variety of responsible ways. For the seventh through ninth graders in your group, we believe that abstinence from sexual intercourse is the best choice. We also recognize that they may want to explore and experience nonpenetrating, safe sexual practices in the years ahead.

The four sessions of this unit offer participants more life skills to make healthy choices. Our hope is that young people will learn to view sexual behavior not merely as penetration/intercourse but as a spectrum of ways to experience a healthy sexuality. We encourage you to be clear but not judgmental in sharing with your group the idea that engaging in sexual intercourse is not a healthy option for young teens. At the same time, we do not condemn those who have made this choice. We do know that everyone will face (or face again) this decision in the future. We want to encourage our young people to engage their hearts and minds, their knowledge, skills, and values, in making healthy choices.

A visit to a local family planning clinic is an optional activity in Session Twenty. We strongly encourage you to choose this option. It is important that youth know what a clinic has to offer them. It is equally important that they feel comfortable approaching the clinic for services in the future. This visit will make a clinic or similar facility more accessible to participants by increasing their levels of knowledge and comfort.

Defining/Redefining Abstinence

R&R (page 201)

Opening Ritual

Set up the centering/focus area before participants arrive. The Unitarian Universalist Principle cards affirming the inherent worth and dignity of every person and justice, equity, and compassion in human relations are appropriate for this session. You may want to include pictures of young people (both other-gender and same-gender) holding hands, kissing, or hugging.

EXPLORING THE THIRD OPTION (page 203)

6. Add the following discussion question:

- What Unitarian Universalist religious values would lead you to make the decision for abstinence? (You may need to help this discussion by sharing your answer to this question.)

DEVIL OR ANGEL (page 204)

8. Add:

- How might your Unitarian Universalist religious values help you stick to your decision to wait for intercourse?

Contraception

We strongly encourage you to take your group on a field trip to a local family planning clinic. If this is not possible, arrange a visit from a representative of a clinic.

In keeping with our Unitarian Universalist values, this session again offers our youth full and accurate information. Make this connection clear to your group, emphasizing that Unitarian Universalism affirms healthy and responsible sexuality and the free and responsible search for truth and meaning. The name of this curriculum is *Our Whole Lives* because we, as Unitarian Universalists, believe that sexuality is an integral part of the totality of life.

R&R (page 211)

Opening Ritual

Set up the centering/focus area before participants arrive. You may want to list in bold letters on a small poster board the name(s) and number(s) of family planning clinics in your area and place the board in the centering area. This reinforces the connection between responsible, healthy sexuality and our respect for the inherent worth and dignity of every person, starting with ourselves.

REFLECTION AND PLANNING FOR NEXT SESSION (page 216)

1. Add:

- How might your religious values as a Unitarian Universalist help you counsel a friend faced with some of the concerns we studied today?

Unintended Pregnancy Options

One of the topics in this session is abortion. Since 1963, the Unitarian Universalist Association (UUA) General Assembly has passed eleven resolutions (1963, 1968, 1973, 1975, 1977, 1978, 1980, 1985, 1986, 1987, 1993) supporting a pro-choice stance. Copies of these resolutions are available from the UUA Faith In Action Department. Men and women in our congregations across the continent have taken part in marches, demonstrations, silent witnessing actions, and lobbying efforts and have volunteered their time, efforts, and money in support of family planning and abortion clinics. In the summer of 1995, James Barrett, a retired military officer and a member of the Unitarian Universalist congregation in Pensacola, Florida, was shot and killed and his wife was injured as they acted as volunteer escorts for a doctor who was entering the abortion clinic in their city. Unitarian Universalists have a long and distinguished history in our support of choice. Our understanding of the issue has deepened over the years. While the 1963 resolution focused on "abortion," the more recent resolutions have focused on "pro-choice," a change that reflects our belief that decisions about pregnancy are complex and that what we support is a woman's right to make these decisions for herself.

In working with younger teens, you may find that some, or even many, of your group members have adopted the anti-abortion stance of neighbors and peers. Young teens are often horrified at the graphic pictures and descriptions used by anti-choice groups. Their own life experiences have not offered them an understanding of the depth and complexity of the issues related to decisions about pregnancy.

Help participants understand that, as Unitarian Universalists, we believe that people have the right to decide ethical and moral issues for themselves. Unitarian Universalists believe that no one has the right to impose his or her values on another's body. This is a concept that can help invite your youth into the next level of understanding of the abortion issue.

R&R (page 229)

Opening Ritual

Set up the centering/focus area before participants arrive. You might include a sign that states that since 1963, the UUA General Assembly has passed eleven pro-choice resolutions. Our first Unitarian Universalist Principle is appropriate for this session. In your time of meditation, you might ask the group to hold in their thoughts all Unitarian Universalists who have stood up for what they believed and, especially, to hold in their thoughts James Barrett, a Unitarian Universalist in Pensacola, Florida, who was shot and killed as he worked as a volunteer at a local clinic.

ATTITUDES TOWARD ABORTION, LEADER RESOURCE 34 (page 234)

Add to Leader Resource 34, Continuum Choice, the statement:

6. Religious institutions should work to create laws that support their beliefs on abortion.

1	2	3	4	5
Absolutely Yes				Absolutely No

Sexual Decisions

Because we value a free and responsible search for truth and meaning, this session offers information and scenarios that are reality-based and explicit. We believe youth need to understand possible sequences of feelings and behaviors in a situation in order to make healthy decisions. Many Unitarian Universalists who took *About Your Sexuality* as young teens report that they were better able to make clear decisions because they had been given complete information.

In each activity in this session, keep in mind the underlying theme that our Unitarian Universalist values and principles can help us make good decisions. Do not overdo this emphasis but be aware of opportunities to gently affirm it.

R&R (page 241)

Opening Ritual

Set up the centering/focus area before participants arrive. You might want to add the Unitarian Universalist Principle cards affirming inherent worth and dignity; justice, equity, and compassion; and free and responsible search for truth and meaning. Consider placing a clock in the centering/focus area as a symbol of taking the time to think through decisions before acting.

REFLECTION AND PLANNING FOR NEXT SESSION (page 244)

1. Add:

- Which Unitarian Universalist values are most relevant to today's session?

Sexually Transmitted Diseases (STDs)

The goal of this unit is the prevention of damaging and life-threatening illnesses. The statistics noted in the core curriculum are alarming: two-thirds of annual reported cases of sexually transmitted diseases are among people under age 25. It is crucial that we offer our youth full information about STDs and STD prevention.

Our young people face very different health challenges than those many of us faced as we approached high school and young adulthood. Participants can use the information and skills in this unit throughout their lives to protect themselves and others and to engage in healthy sexual practices. We have much anecdotal information to indicate that when our Unitarian Universalist youth reach young adulthood, they often serve as informal sources of accurate information for friends who did not have the benefit of a comprehensive sexuality education program. Thus, the information you share in this unit will truly be lifesaving for countless numbers of people over the years to come.

STD Facts

The Unitarian Universalist Principles of the inherent worth and dignity of every person and justice, equity, and compassion in human relations are important as you present some alarming facts in this session. We believe it is important that people have accurate and full information about sexually transmitted infections. It is also important that people with STDs be treated with justice, equity, and compassion.

R&R (page 260)

Opening Ritual

Set up the centering/focusing area before the participants arrive. Appropriate Unitarian Universalist Principle cards include the inherent worth and dignity of every person and justice, equity, and compassion in human relations.

REFLECTION AND PLANNING FOR NEXT SESSION (page 263)

Add the following discussion questions:

- How has your congregation responded to people with HIV/AIDS? Has there been any outreach? If participants do not know, decide as a group how they can find out during the week (talk with the minister or religious educator, call the chair of the social action/outreach committee, etc.). Do they know of any other congregations (Unitarian Universalist or other denomination) that offer outreach in your community?

STD Prevention

This session includes lifesaving skills and information for STD prevention. The condom activities may seem premature for the sexual activity level of the majority of your participants. However, if our young teens can be comfortable with condoms now in a setting that does not involve peer pressure and the stresses of an intimate relationship, they will be more likely to use the appropriate skills and knowledge when they are needed.

Our Unitarian Universalist congregations can play an important role in encouraging local communities to provide youth with access to condoms. In one New England town, youth were sent to the local drugstore to find out where condoms were located and how easy or difficult it would be to purchase them. They discovered that the condoms were easy to find, but a store employee refused to sell them to teens. One of the ministers of the congregation then visited the drugstore and talked with the manager. The manager agreed that in the future, the store would sell condoms to anyone who asked for them. The youth learned that a leader of their religious community was a person they could turn to with justice issues related to healthy and safe sexuality.

R&R (page 280)

Opening Ritual

Set up the centering/focus area before participants arrive. The Unitarian Universalist Principle card affirming justice, equity, and compassion in human relations is appropriate for this session.

PLANNING A CELEBRATION (page 283)

Ask the group if they would like to share their closing celebration in some way with the congregation. For example, they may want to make statements about their experiences in the program as part of a Sunday worship service, an intergenerational event, or in written form in the newsletter.

REFLECTION AND PLANNING FOR NEXT SESSION (page 284)

1. Add the following:

- Ask the group, "Can youth buy condoms easily at drugstores in our area?" After you have heard their responses, suggest that they (individually or in small groups) visit a local drugstore to try to buy condoms. Share with them the story about the New England Unitarian Universalist congregation described earlier. If you or your minister or religious educator are willing to intervene in the same way, tell participants that if they find stores where they are not permitted to buy condoms, positive actions will be taken.

Abuse of Sexuality

The two sessions of this unit focus on a topic that is extremely important and difficult to talk about for many people. The abuse of sexuality has occurred throughout human history. We are now more able and willing to stand up and name it, to declare it wrong, to offer healing for its victims, and to offer preventive strategies for children, youth, and adults. Violence and abuse come from deep-seated pain and fear expressed in destructive ways. It is important for us to have the courage to help bring the light of understanding and compassion to those who have been affected by sexual abuse.

The Unitarian Universalist Principles of the inherent worth and dignity of every individual and justice, equity, and compassion in human relations offer courage to our children, youth, and adults. A resource for Unitarian Universalist congregations is *Creating Safe Congregations: Toward an Ethic of Right Relations*, available from the Unitarian Universalist Association Bookstore. This resource includes a restatement of Unitarian Universalist Principles as they relate to the issues of sexual abuse and violence. You may want to make copies of this statement for participants, or you may want to place a copy in the centering/focus area for your opening ritual. (You will find a copy on the next page.) It affirms for your group that their religious community is a place that offers support and healing for these painful challenges.

It is very important to know the policies of your congregation and religious education program regarding suspected sexual abuse. You need to know the reporting laws of your state or province, the procedures in your congregation, and the role of your minister(s). Talk with your minister or religious educator about these issues.

This unit may save a life someday. It will be challenging to teach, but the understanding and strategies offered to your students will benefit them throughout their lives. Their understanding and compassion related to sexual abuse will help them help others prevent destructive patterns of behavior. Slowly but certainly, the tide of violence will diminish and perhaps someday stop.

Unitarian Universalist Principles and Sexual Ethics

The inherent worth and dignity of every person

Every person's sexuality is sacred and is worthy of respect; therefore, it is not to be violated.

Justice, equity, and compassion in human relations

We treat others as we would want to be treated; therefore, sexual exploitation and interpersonal violence are wrong.

Acceptance of one another and encouragement to spiritual growth

Accepting each other as we are means doing no harm and fostering well-being in one's self and others.

A free and responsible search for truth and meaning

In our relationship to others, our freedom of sexuality is as important as the responsibility for it.

The right of conscience and the use of the democratic process within our congregations and society at large

As a community and an institution, we are responsible for creating a secure, safe, and nonviolent environment.

The goal of a world community with peace, liberty, and justice for all

We have the opportunity to create the kind of environment that lends itself to peace, liberty, and justice in human interactions, and we can become a model for the rest of society.

Respect for the interdependent web of *all* existence of which we are a part

When we respect each person's sexual integrity, we honor the wholeness of life and respect the web of all existence.

Recovering from Sexual Abuse

R&R (page 295)

Opening Ritual

Set up the centering/focus area before participants arrive. The Unitarian Universalist Principle cards affirming inherent worth and dignity and justice, equity, and compassion might be used for this session. A copy of Unitarian Universalist Principles and Sexual Ethics could be framed and added to the focus area or made into a poster for the wall.

You may want to begin by handing out copies of Unitarian Universalist Principles and Sexual Ethics to each participant. This handout could serve as an opening reading with one leader reading the Unitarian Universalist Principle and different participants reading the statements that relate the Principle to sexual ethics.

COPING STRATEGIES (page 296)

2. Add to strategies for avoiding or dealing with abuse:
   - Talk with your minister or religious educator or a trusted member in your congregation.

REFLECTION AND PLANNING FOR NEXT SESSION (page 297)

1. Add to sharing:
   - What Unitarian Universalist values are relevant to this session?

Sexual Harassment and Acquaintance Rape

In preparing for this session, ask your minister, religious educator, or president of your congregation if your congregation has a statement related to harassment, abuse, or rape. If it does, make copies for your group.

R&R (page 314)

Opening Ritual

Set up the centering/focus area before participants arrive. The Unitarian Universalist principles cards affirming inherent worth and dignity and justice, equity, and compassion might be used for this session. You may want to again place a copy of Unitarian Universalist Principles and Sexual Ethics in the focus area. You might divide the group in half and have one half read the Unitarian Universalist Principle and the other half read the statement relating the principle to sexual ethics.

If your congregation has a written policy related to harassment, abuse, or rape, tell the group you will distribute a copy of that policy later in this session.

SEXUAL HARASSMENT: ASSESSING THE IMPACT (page 316)

5. Add to the discussion questions:

- Have you seen incidents of sexual harassment in your congregation? In your group?
- What would be a good way to respond to sexual harassment in your congregation?
- If you were at a conference with other Unitarian Universalist youth and witnessed sexual harassment, what could you do?

MYTHINFORMATION GAME: RAPE (page 318)

8. Add:

- Add to the list of local resources participants could turn to, "talk with your minister or religious educator."

REFLECTION AND PLANNING FOR NEXT SESSION (page 320)

If your congregation has a written harassment or abuse policy, hand out copies to participants.

1. Ask:

- How can our religious community help you respond to situations of harassment and rape?

Celebration and Closure

This concluding session is a chance for you and your group to reflect on your experiences together, your learnings, your new sense of self, and your identity as Unitarian Universalists.

Session Twenty-seven suggests several closure activities, but it is intended to be a participatory session designed by the whole group.

Here are a few additional suggestions that relate the program to religious community:

- As part of their closing, ask your group, "Why is it important that we did this program in our congregation?" Record their responses on newsprint. *If* the group is comfortable with the idea, share their responses with the board of your congregation, the Religious Education Committee, and/or the congregation as a whole. Adults in the congregation will benefit from hearing the youths' responses to this question and will likely feel a greater commitment to comprehensive sexuality education and a sense a pride in their congregation for offering such a program.
- Have each participant create a memento or symbol that reflects her or his sense of Unitarian Universalist identity, especially as it may have been strengthened through this program. You may also choose to give a memento to each participant to reflect this growth.
- Share how your Unitarian Universalist values and commitment have been strengthened by your participation in this program. You have become a role model for your youth, and your sharing is an optimal learning opportunity for them.

Finally, thank you for your energy, enthusiasm, creativity, and commitment to the youth in this program. You have truly offered your young people a better and more healthy future.

We affirm and promote . . .

the inherent worth and dignity
of every person.

We affirm and promote . . .

the inherent worth and dignity
of every person.

We affirm and promote . . .

justice, equity, and compassion
in human relations.

We affirm and promote . . .

justice, equity, and compassion
in human relations.

We affirm and promote . . .

acceptance of one another and encouragement to spiritual growth in our congregations.

We affirm and promote . . .

acceptance of one another and encouragement to spiritual growth in our congregations.

We affirm and promote . . .

a free and responsible search
for truth and meaning.

We affirm and promote . . .

a free and responsible search
for truth and meaning.

We affirm and promote . . .

the right of conscience and
the use of the democratic process
in our congregations and
in society at large.

We affirm and promote . . .

the right of conscience and
the use of the democratic process
in our congregations and
in society at large.

We affirm and promote . . .

the goal of world community
with peace, liberty, and justice
for all.

We affirm and promote . . .

the goal of world community
with peace, liberty, and justice
for all.

We affirm and promote . . .

respect for the interdependent web of all existence of which we are a part.

We affirm and promote . . .

respect for the interdependent
web of all existence of which
we are a part.

United Church of Christ

Sexuality and Our Faith

A Companion to Our Whole Lives

Grades 7–9

Reverend Lizann Bassham
Reverend Gordon J. Svoboda II

Introduction to the United Church of Christ Companion

As Christians, we profess that we are created in the image of God. In this image, we make a lifelong journey toward deeper faith, faithfulness, and wholeness. As a church, we seek continually to integrate God's ongoing revelation with new knowledge and understandings of our lives and times. In our religious education, we seek to equip the faithful for this journey in all its possibilities.

As people in the United Church of Christ, we affirm that sexuality and spirituality are intricately connected and that both are gifts from God. The actions of our General Synods, conferences, associations, congregations, and councils support this. We do not believe that "sexuality is a gift of God; just don't talk about it in church!"

Sexuality education and ministries have been important to the United Church of Christ since the denomination's early days. The actions of General Synods, the Executive Council, and other councils of the church bear proof to this commitment. Our actions have been pastoral and prophetic. We have focused on both the persons and the social policies.

In the 1960s, with the lead of the United Church of Christ Council for Christian Social Action, the denomination turned its attention to issues of overpopulation and the need for access to family planning resources. Since the mid-1960s, it has focused on the ethical and faith issues involved in family planning and freedom of choice in pregnancy. This dialogue and study resulted in the 1971 Eighth General Synod's resolution, "Freedom of Choice Concerning Abortion," which supported freedom of choice.

In 1969, the Council for Christian Social Action called for an end to discrimination against gays and lesbians and challenged the denomination to work toward justice for all people suffering the pain of homophobia. Three years later, the United Church of Christ became the first Protestant denomination to acknowledge the ordination of an openly gay man. Since 1969, national United Church of Christ decision-making bodies have endorsed no less than twelve actions calling for the support of gay, lesbian, and bisexual persons in our churches and society.

Equality of women and men is another pastoral and prophetic mission of the United Church of Christ. In 1975, the United Church of Christ Task Force on Women in Church and Society called upon the denomination to undertake a comprehensive study of human sexuality. This study resulted in the publication of *Human Sexuality: A Preliminary Study* (United Church of Christ. New York: United Church Press, 1977), which was presented to the denomination at the 1977 General Synod. This document was ahead of its time and continues to serve as a guidepost to the United Church of Christ and to other religious organizations.

Groups studied the report in a variety of settings in the United Church of Christ. As a result, in 1983 General Synod asked the United Church Board for Homeland Ministries to provide additional sexuality resources to local congregations and conferences. The Board surveyed local church members about their faith and sexuality-related needs and stories. Among many important findings, 83 percent of the people responding to the survey stated their conviction that the church has a responsibility to teach sexuality education. The majority also wanted the church to provide guidance in decision making on sexuality issues and to assist in recovery from hurtful experiences. The survey findings were the basis for the adult sexuality education resource, *Created in God's Image: A Human Sexuality Program for Ministry and Mission* (Melanie Morrison and Eleanor S. Morrison. Cleveland: United Church Board for Homeland Ministries, 1993), and for this series, *Our Whole Lives*.

This supplement will put the exploration of identity, relationships, and sexuality in the context of worship and our relationship with God and scripture. The goals are to connect faith with identity, relationships, and sexuality issues in ways that lead to informed and reasoned decisions and to empower persons to act responsibly as they seek to unite body and spirit, spirituality and sexuality, alienation and wholeness.

The following principles from *Created in God's Image: A Human Sexuality Program for Ministry and Mission*, Participant's Book, pp. 6-8, supplement the *Our Whole Lives* assumptions, goals, and principles. They are a good presentation of what many in the United Church of Christ believe about faith, spirituality, sexuality, and justice.

Principles Guiding the United Church of Christ Commitment to Sexuality Education

All of us are sexual beings, whether we are young or old; married, unmarried, or celibate; widowed or divorced; able-bodied or physically disabled. It is sometimes erroneously assumed that sexual feelings begin with puberty and diminish as one approaches old age. In fact, our sexual responses begin in the womb, quickly grow to include sexual feelings, and both remain a vital part of our experience until we die. We experience pleasurable bodily sensations that can be called sexual from infancy on. Researcher Mary Calderone notes that "one of the earliest things a boy baby does after the first cry is to have an erection; the girl baby's vagina lubricates within twenty-four hours of birth."[1] Elderly people, just as much as young and middle-aged people, have sexual feelings, desires, and needs for intimacy.

Recalling the expansiveness of the term *sexuality* and affirming that to be human is to be sexual, the authors wish to make explicit nine assumptions that underlie these sessions. In articulating these assumptions, it is not presumed that participants in these sessions will necessarily agree with every assumption. The hope is that these assumptions will help participants reflect upon the personal convictions they bring to this study of human sexuality.

1. Sexuality is a God-given gift.

God created every one of use with the capacity to respond to, and be in relationship with, others and the world around us.One of the vital dimensions of this capacity is our sexuality. We are physical as well as spiritual and intellectual beings, and we have senses through which we can delight in the beauty of creation. As the early chapters of Genesis affirm, God looked upon all that was created and declared that it is good. Our sexuality, no less than any other part of this created world, can express this goodness.

2. The purposes of sexuality are to enhance human wholeness and fulfillment, to express love, commitment, delight, and pleasure, to bring new life into the world, and to give glory to God.

Understanding sexuality as a gift from God means that this dimension of our humanity is given us for a purpose. Sexuality is a gift that calls us to wholeness as individuals. We know the costs to ourselves as persons when we neglect or abuse our bodies. We also know the pleasure and joy available to us when we care for our bodies and our health.

Another purpose of sexuality is to express love for and delight in another human being. Joy and pleasure are to be shared, and sexual expression in the context of a loving relationship is one way of sharing. Sexuality can be a wellspring of creativity, including the procreation of new life, but sexual activity can also be affirmed and celebrated apart from procreation. Because it brings us into relationship with others and with the world, sexuality can be a means of giving glory to God.

1. Mary S. Calderone, "Eroticism as a Norm," *The Family Coordinator* (October 1974):338.

3. When making decisions about sexuality, the primary guide is God's call to love and justice as revealed in both Testaments.

As Christians, we look to the scriptures as the primary guide of knowing how God's Spirit moves in our midst. In matters of human sexuality, we do not limit our study of the scriptures to those passages where words such as *sex*, *marriage*, and *divorce* are found. The great biblical themes of creation, exodus, incarnation, resurrection, love, and justice can inform our discussions and decision making about human sexuality.

At the heart of the Torah, the Prophets, and the Gospels is the call to love God, neighbors, and ourselves, and to serve justice in human relationships and society. No valid interpretation can ignore, or contradict, this call to love and justice.

To say that the Bible is the primary source of inspiration and knowledge for Christians does not mean that it is the only one. Our understanding of human sexuality can be deepened and enriched when we avail ourselves of accurate and up-to-date information and research. We affirm the reality of the living Spirit that moves where it will and is as active in our day as in the days when the scriptures were recorded.

4. From a biblical perspective, sexuality is intended to express mutuality, love, and justice. In judging whether behavior is ethical or unethical, the norms of mutuality, love, and justice are the central criteria.

The scriptures call us to affirm the essential goodness of human sexuality as part of God's creation. This God-given gift can be exercised responsibly in behavior that expresses mutuality, love, and justice. The gift can also be abused. Because we have the freedom to behave responsibly or irresponsibly, we are also accountable for our behavior.

5. From a biblical perspective, sexuality is distorted by unethical behaviors, attitudes, and systems that foster violence, exploitation, infidelity, assertion of power, and the treatment of persons as objects.

The gift of sexuality is distorted and abused whenever the worth and well-being of a human being is undermined. Distortion can occur in interpersonal relationships when commitment is violated, power is abused, or a person is treated as an object. Social, political, and economic injustices also contribute to the distortion of sexuality. Racism and sexism are grounded in fundamental distortions that assert that some people have the right to dominate and control others.

6. In developing a just sexual morality, we need to avoid double standards.

In matters of sexual morality, a double standard has too often been employed. Women (and girls), for example, have been expected to conform to different sexual norms and behavior than men (and boys). There has been much attention given to the immorality of pre-marital and extra-marital conduct, but too little attention given to what constitutes immoral behavior within marriage.

As stated previously, all relationships are subject to the same criteria of ethical assessment—the degree to which the persons and relationships reflect mutuality, love, and justice.[2] These ethical criteria ought to form a single standard by which we judge appropriate or inappropriate sexual behavior. There should not be one standard for males, another for females; one for married persons, another for single persons; one for heterosexuals, another for homosexuals; one for the young, another for older persons; one for the able-bodied, another for people with physical and mental disabilities.

7. A responsible and mature sexual ethic respects the moral agency of every person.

When faced with ethical decisions, each of us needs to be accorded the freedom and responsibility to choose. We may turn to the scriptures, call upon the Spirit in prayer, and invite the counsel of trusted people as we seek to discern what is right to do. But finally, each of us must choose and bear the consequences of her or his choice. Without human freedom there cannot be genuine moral responsibility. If the freedom of choice is curtailed, our power as self-defining moral agents is undermined. Therefore, a responsible and mature sexual ethic will respect and protect the freedom of belief and choice.

8. The church, at all levels, ought to be a context for discussion about human sexuality.

Responsible choice about sexual matters is at the heart of the Christian life. Therefore, the Christian community is obliged to provide information and opportunities for understanding the choices we face. Unfortunately, open and informed discussion about sexuality occurs too seldom in our churches. This silence results in unnecessary pain and isolation.

We affirm the efforts of congregations, associations, conferences, and instrumentalities to provide resources for all age groups, train leaders to facilitate discussions about sexuality, and develop programs in the area of human sexuality.

2. For the wording of these criteria for ethical assessment, we are indebted to the "Report of the Task Force on Changing Patterns of Sexuality and Family Life," prepared for the Episcopal Diocese of Newark. This report is published in John Spong's book, Living in Sin? (San Francisco: Harper & Row, 1988), 230–248.

9. The church ought to encourage and support advocacy with those who are sexually oppressed or the victims of sexual violence and abuse. The church can and must have a role in defining and implementing public policy.

Christians are called to shape a civic community in which justice and human well-being prevail. That calling means that we stand in solidarity with the oppressed, including the sexually oppressed, and that we work for the enactment of just laws and the just distribution of resources.[3]

Sexuality education and ministries have been important to the United Church of Christ since the denomination's early days. The actions of General Synods, the Executive Council, and other councils and agencies of the church bear the proof of this commitment. Our actions have been pastoral and prophetic. We have focused on the persons and the social policies.

This companion volume will put the exploration of identity, relationships, and sexuality in the context of worship and our relationship with God and scripture. The goal is to connect faith with identity, relationships, and sexuality issues in ways that lead to informed and reasoned decisions and then empower persons to act responsibly as they seek to unit body and spirit, spirituality and sexuality, alienation and wholeness.

DESIGN AND USE OF THIS COMPANION

The worship services for the beginning and the closing of the curriculum invite participants to covenant with God and with each other to explore and question, to learn and grow throughout the program and into the future. The goal of these and the worship times during individual units and sessions is to further connect the program values and spiritual/religious values.

The unit opening worship can serve as an ongoing link, if you choose, by being repeated at the beginning of each session. A copy of the opening worship follows this section and can be photocopied.

Unit closing worships reflect the themes discussed in the unit. Units Four, Five, Six, and Seven and Units Eight, Nine, and Ten are grouped together with one closing worship for each group. The worship materials explain the rationale for putting the units together. Closing worship services are located in the supplement at the end of each unit or group and can be photocopied for use.

Since each unit has an opening worship service, additional worship time is not included in a unit's first session. Likewise, there is not a separate closing worship for the last session in a unit.

3. *Created In God's Image, A Human Sexuality Program for Ministry and Mission*, Melanie Morrison and Eleanor S. Morrison (Cleveland: United Church Board for Homeland Ministries, 1993) pp. 6–8. Used with permission.

Suggestions for integrating scripture and worship themes into the sessions are made throughout the resource. When multiple points can be emphasized throughout the unit, tips are the same for each session in that unit.

A Note about the Music Resources

You will find most of the suggested music in two resources, *The New Century Hymnal* (Cleveland: Pilgrim Press, 1995) and *The Tune Book* (San Anselmo, CA: Songs and Creations, 1994). Suggested songs and chants not in either of these are printed in this supplement. If other songs or pieces are more appropriate to your situation and group, feel free to substitute them.

Opening Worship for Each Unit and Session

Preparing for this worship: Arrange the room before the participants arrive. In the center of the room, set up a low table covered with brightly colored fabric. Place five candles in holders on the table and have matches or a lighter handy. Ask for volunteers to read the various voices in this service.

Gathering Chant: The New Century Hymnal #742

Litany

(Have someone light a candle as each of the program values is lifted up.)

VOICE ONE: Why have we come together?

ALL: We come to worship God in whose image we were created—spiritual physical beings.

VOICE ONE: God gifted us with bodies and emotions to express our spirituality in concrete ways. One of the ways we affirm the sacredness of life is through healthy sexuality.

ALL: Let us celebrate God's gift of incarnation and affirm our desire for sexual health and the joy it brings.

(Light a candle.)

VOICE TWO: In the beginning, God gave humanity life and blessed us. God continues to bless each of us individually.

ALL: Let us celebrate God's gift and remember our own self-worth.

(Light a candle.)

VOICE TWO: God gifted us with free will—the ability to make our own decisions.

ALL: Let us celebrate God's guidance and help as we struggle with this wonderful and awesome responsibility.

(Light a candle.)

VOICE ONE: The God in whose image we are created is a God of justice.

ALL: Let us answer that call for justice in our own lives and relationships.

(Light a candle.)

VOICE TWO: The God in whose image we are created is a God of diversity.

ALL: Let us celebrate that diversity by working to include all people regardless of their gender, physical differences, sexual orientation, age, race, and other things that make us different from one another.

(Light a candle.)

VOICE ONE: Let us pray:

ALL: God of touch and taste, sight and sound, aromas and delight, thank you for giving us the breath of life. Thank you for your blessings on us as fully human beings. Help us to use our gifts as we work with you to bring more joy and justice into your world. Help us to delight in our differences and to welcome each other into this amazing world you created for us. Amen.

Worship Service for the Beginning of the Curriculum

This worship service is designed for use at the beginning of the program. Leaders are encouraged to involve parents/guardians and participants in the worship experience. Arrange the room before the participants arrive. In the center of the room, set up a low table covered with brightly colored fabric. Place five candles in holders on the table and have matches or a lighter handy. Ask for volunteers to read the various voices in this service. Be sure there is a mix of youth and adults serving as readers.

Gathering Chant: The New Century Hymnal #742

Litany

(Have someone light a candle as each of the program values is lifted up.)

VOICE ONE: Why have we come together?

ALL: We come to worship God in whose image we were created—spiritual physical beings.

VOICE ONE: God gifted us with bodies and emotions to express our spirituality in concrete ways. One of the ways we affirm the sacredness of life is through healthy sexuality.

ALL: Let us celebrate God's gift of incarnation and affirm our desire for sexual health and the joy it brings.

(Light a candle.)

VOICE TWO: In the beginning, God gave humanity life and blessed us. God continues to bless each of us individually.

ALL: Let us celebrate God's gift and remember our own self-worth.

(Light a candle.)

VOICE TWO: God gifted us with free will—the ability to make our own decisions.

ALL: Let us celebrate God's guidance and help as we struggle with this wonderful and awesome responsibility.

(Light a candle.)

VOICE ONE: The God in whose image we are created is a God of justice.

ALL: Let us answer that call for justice in our own lives and relationships.

(Light a candle.)

VOICE TWO: The God in whose image we are created is a God of diversity.

ALL: Let us celebrate that diversity by working to include all people regardless of their gender, physical differences, sexual orientation, age, race, and other things that make us different from one another.

(Light a candle.)

VOICE ONE: Let us pray:

ALL: God of touch and taste, sight and sound, aromas and delight, thank you for giving us the breath of life. Thank your for your blessings on us as fully human beings. Help us to use our gifts as we work with you to bring more joy and justice into your world. Help us to delight in our differences and to welcome each other into this amazing world you created for us. Amen.

Song Celebrating Our Being Part of the Body of Christ: "Many Are the Lightbeams," The New Century Hymnal #163

Scripture Reading: Romans 12:4–8 and 1 Corinthians 12:12–13

VOICE ONE: We live out our spirituality in sacred bodies, and together we are the body of Christ. Hear how the apostle Paul describes it in Romans 12:4–8:

VOICE TWO: "For as in one body we have many members, and not all the members have the same function, so we, who are many, are one body in Christ, and individually we are members one of another."

VOICE THREE: "We have gifts that differ according to the grace given to us: prophecy, in proportion to faith; ministry, in ministering; the teacher, in teaching; the exhorter, in exhortation; the giver, in generosity; the leader, in diligence; the compassionate, in cheerfulness."

VOICE ONE: And in 1 Corinthians 12:12–13, Paul writes:

VOICE TWO: "For just as the body is one and has many members, and all the members of the body, though many, are one body, so it is with Christ. For in the one Spirit we were all baptized into one body—Jews or Greeks, slaves or free—and we were all made to drink of one Spirit."

COVENANTING WITH GOD AND EACH OTHER TO EXPLORE WHAT IT MEANS TO BE SPIRITUAL PHYSICAL BEINGS

VOICE ONE: Throughout this program, we will explore and learn about many topics. Will you promise to listen to your own thoughts and words as you explore what you think and believe, and in so doing, learn about yourself?

(Allow a few moments of silence while each participant decides if they can commit to that.)

VOICE ONE: If you are willing, please respond:

PARTICIPANTS (including adults): I will, with the help of God.

VOICE TWO: Will you promise to listen to the ideas and thoughts of others, and in so doing, learn about each other?

(Allow a few moments of silence while each participant decides if they can commit to that.)

VOICE TWO: If you are willing, please respond:

PARTICIPANTS (including adults): I will, with the help of God.

VOICE THREE: We are sacred, spiritual physical beings. Everything we do with our bodies is an opportunity to show, in a concrete way, the image of God in which we were created and to show that we are part of the Body of Christ. Will you promise to look for those connections in this program and to ask questions if you do not see the connection?

(Allow a few moments of silence while each participant decides if they can commit to that.)

VOICE THREE: If you are willing, please respond:

PARTICIPANTS (including adults): I will, with the help of God.

VOICE ONE: Let us pray:

ALL: God, thank you for making us in your image. Thank you for making us part of the Body of Christ. Help us keep our promises as we learn more about ourselves, each other, you, and especially who we are as sacred, spiritual physical beings. Amen.

Closing Song: "Blessed Be the Tie That Binds," v. 1,* The New Century Hymnal *#393

BENEDICTION

Go now and learn, listen, explore, and grow.

Group Building and Examining Values

SESSION ONE

Introduction to the Program

Use Opening Worship for each Unit and Session (hereafter referred to as Unit or Session Opening Worship).

Examining Values

SESSION OPENING WORSHIP

Tips for integrating scripture and worship concepts into Session 2

During the various exercises in Session 2, everyone will have an opportunity to share and explore different feelings and values. Let the group know that being different from one another is the way God made us. We are all part of the Body of Christ; however, like different parts of the body, we each see the world in different ways. The apostle Paul used that image a lot in his writings.

As leaders, you will set the tone for the rest of the sessions through your first interactions with the group. As values and feelings are explored and the group is being formed, your expressions of open and nonjudgmental encouragement and sharing are important.

Unit One Closing Worship

A SERVICE TO HONOR OUR DIVERSITY AND UNITY

Preparing for this worship: Ask for volunteers to read the various voices in this service.

Song Celebrating Our Different Feelings and Values: "Part of the Family" by Jim Manley (p. 113 of this volume).

Scripture Reading: 1 Corinthians 12:14–26

VOICE ONE: Many of us have the same feelings and values. Many of us have different feelings and values. All our feelings and values are part of who we are as the Body of Christ. It is in the Body of Christ that we unite in our differences. The apostle Paul writes in 1 Corinthians:

VOICE TWO: "Indeed, the body does not consist of one member but of many. If the foot would say, 'Because I am not a hand, I do not belong to the body,' that would not make it any less a part of the body. And if the ear would say, 'Because I am not an eye, I do not belong to the body,' that would not make it any less a part of the body."

VOICE THREE: "If the whole body were an eye, where would the hearing be? If the whole body were hearing, where would the sense of smell be? But as it is, God arranged the members in the body, each one of them, as God chose. If all were a single member, where would the body be?"

MAKING THE BODY OF CHRIST

VOICE ONE: If one side of the room were the top of the head of the body of Christ and the other side were the bottom of the feet of the body of Christ and all the space in between were the different parts of the body, which part would you be? Get up and move to where you would be in the body of Christ.

(Let everyone move into the formation of the Body.)

VOICE TWO: Starting with the people at the top of the head, if you are willing to share what part you are and why, please do so.

(Allow time for sharing.)

VOICE THREE: Let us pray:

ALL: God who made us all, thank you for all the feelings and values we have in common and also for those about which we disagree. Help us to continue to grow together as the Body of Christ. Amen.

Closing Song: "Part of the Family," v. 1, by Jim Manley

BENEDICTION

Go and be a spiritual physical being. Laugh and cry, be angry at injustice, and be compassionate and tender with those who are vulnerable. Discover what you value and be true to your beliefs. Remember that, as a child of God, you are accountable to God and to each other for all that you do.

Part of the Family

For Judy Wagner and Tim

Words and music by
JIM MANLEY

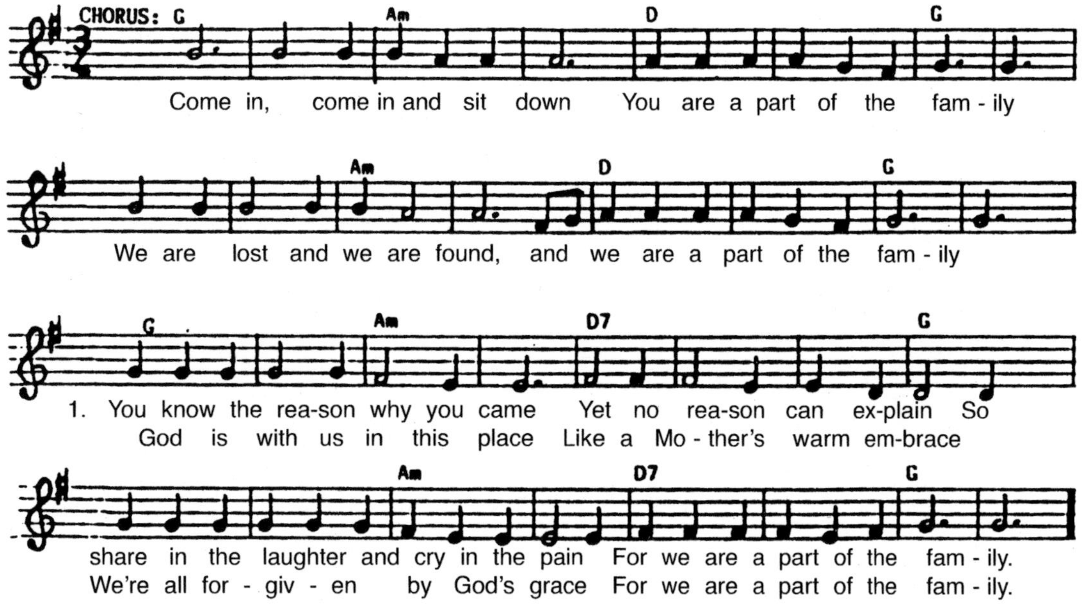
CHORUS: G
Am
D
G
Come in, come in and sit down You are a part of the fam - ily
Am
D
G
We are lost and we are found, and we are a part of the fam - ily
G
Am
D7
G
1. You know the rea-son why you came Yet no rea-son can ex-plain So
God is with us in this place Like a Mo - ther's warm em-brace
Am
D7
G
share in the laughter and cry in the pain For we are a part of the fam - ily.
We're all for - giv - en by God's grace For we are a part of the fam - ily.

2. Children and elders, middlers and teens
Singles and doubles and in-betweens
Strong 85'ers and street-wise sixteens
We are a part of the family.

Greeters and shoppers, long-time and new
Nobody here has a claim on a pew.
And whether we're many or only a few
We are a part of the family.

3. There's life to be shared in the bread and the wine
We are the branches, Christ is the vine
This is God's temple, it's not yours or mine
But we are a part of the family.

There's rest for the weary, and health for us all
There's a yoke that is easy and a burden that's small
So come in and worship and answer the call
For we are a part of the family.

Sexuality and Body Awareness

SESSION THREE

Sexual Language

UNIT OPENING WORSHIP

Tips for integrating scripture and worship concepts into Session 3

During the Breaking the Language Barrier exercise, you can reaffirm Genesis 1:26–31. God created humankind in God's own image. God also blessed us and called us good. That blessing and goodness include our sexuality, genitalia, and sexual orientation.

SESSION 3 CLOSING

Closing Song: (to the tune of the Doxology)

Praise God for all we hear and see.
Praise God for smells of earth and sea.
Praise God for things to eat and touch.
Praise God for blessing us so much.

BENEDICTION

Go now and enjoy God's good creation. Go now and know that you are also part of God's good creation! Hear, smell, taste, touch, and see the goodness in and around you!

Anatomy and Physiology

SESSION OPENING WORSHIP

Tips for integrating worship and scripture concepts into Session 4

During the Anatomy and Physiology Cards and Constructing Sexual Systems exercises in Session 4, you can reaffirm Genesis 1:26–31. God created humankind in God's own image. God also blessed us and called us good. That blessing and goodness include our sexuality, genitalia, and sexual orientation.

The closing worship after the next session requires a bit of homework. Ask all the participants to bring to next week's service something they particularly enjoy that symbolizes the goodness of creation, especially something that includes a sensual experience. Someone who loves to play or hear music could bring an instrument or a CD or could sing a bit at the appointed time. Someone could bring ice cream, chocolate, a flower that smells especially wonderful to him or her, or something visually appealing, etc.

SESSION 4 CLOSING

Closing Song: (to the tune of the Doxology)

Praise God for all we hear and see.
Praise God for smells of earth and sea.
Praise God for things to eat and touch.
Praise God for blessing us so much.

BENEDICTION

Go now and enjoy God's good creation. Go now and know that you are also part of God's good creation! Hear, smell, taste, touch, and see the goodness in and around you!

Personal Concerns about Puberty

SESSION OPENING WORSHIP

Tips for integrating scripture and worship concepts into Session 5

In the exercises Am I Normal? and Personal Concerns of Boys and Girls, you can reaffirm Genesis 1:26–31. God created humankind in God's own image. God also blessed us and called us good. That blessing and goodness include our sexuality, genitalia, and sexual orientation.

Unit Two Closing Worship

A WORSHIP SERVICE TO CELEBRATE THE GIFT OF OUR BODIES AND SEXUALITY

Preparing for this worship: Allow time for participants who did not bring something to draw a picture or representation of something that symbolizes the goodness of creation to them.

Song Celebrating the Goodness of Creation (choose one):
"*All Things Bright and Beautiful,*" The New Century Hymnal *#31;*
"*Cantemos al Creador,*" The New Century Hymnal *#39;*
"*Colorful Creator,*" The New Century Hymnal *#30;*
"*I Sing the Mighty Power of God,*" The New Century Hymnal *#12.*

Scripture Reading: Selections from Genesis 1:1–31

VOICE ONE: "In the beginning when God created the heavens and the earth…God said, 'Let there be light'; and there was light."

ALL: "And God saw that the light was good!"

VOICE TWO: "And God separated…the waters from the waters…And God said, 'Let the waters under the sky be gathered together into one place, and let the dry land appear.' And it was so. God called the dry land Earth, and the waters that were gathered together God called Seas."

ALL: "And God saw that it was good!"

VOICE THREE: "Then God said, 'Let the earth put forth vegetation: plants yielding seed, and fruit trees of every kind on earth that bear fruit with the seed in it.' And it was so…"

ALL: "And God saw that it was good!"

VOICE ONE: "And God said, 'Let there be lights in the dome of the sky to separate the day from the night.'…. God made the two great lights…and the stars…."

ALL: "And God saw that it was good!"

VOICE TWO: "And God said, 'Let the waters bring forth swarms of living creatures, and let birds fly above the earth across the dome of the sky.'…"

ALL: "And God saw that it was good!"

VOICE THREE: "And God said, 'Let the earth bring forth living creatures of every kind....' And it was so...."

ALL: "And God saw that it was good!"

VOICE ONE: "Then God said, 'Let us make humankind in our image, according to our likeness....' So God created humankind in God's own image, in the image of God they were created; male and female they were created."

VOICE TWO: "God blessed them...."

VOICE THREE: "God saw everything that God had made."

ALL: "And indeed, it was very good!!"

OFFERING OUR THANKS FOR THE GOODNESS OF CREATION

VOICE ONE: Each of us experiences the goodness of creation in different ways. Some people enjoy music more than anything, or the taste of chocolate, or the feel of a close and loving hug. I invite each of you to come forward with your symbol of the goodness of creation. If you wish to, say what it is and why it is important to you and put it on the table. If it would work, share it with the group, especially if it is chocolate or a hug. After each person finishes, we will all say, "Thank you God for [whatever the symbol is]."

(Go around the circle and share the symbols.)

Closing Song: (to the tune of the Doxology)

Praise God for all we hear and see.
Praise God for smells of earth and sea.
Praise God for things to eat and touch.
Praise God for blessing us so much.

BENEDICTION

Go now and enjoy God's good creation. Go now and know that you are also part of God's good creation! Hear, smell, taste, touch, and see the goodness in and around you!

Gender and Diversity

SESSION SIX

Understanding Gender Roles

UNIT OPENING WORSHIP

Tips for integrating scripture and worship concepts into Session 6

There are many times during the various exercises in Sessions 6 and 7 when you can lift up how Jesus welcomed and valued all persons, especially those outcast or shunned by others:

the poor widow (Luke 21:1–4)
the Good Samaritan (Luke 10:29–37)
the sinner who anointed Jesus' feet (Luke 7:36–50)

A number of exercises in Session 6 point out the way in which society stereotypes males and females and puts us all in boxes. Remind participants what scripture says in Galatians 3:28: In Christ we are neither male nor female; we are all equal. Remind them that all of humankind—male and female—is created in God's image (Genesis 1:27). When they think about the images of humans presented in society, do those images honor the image of God in which we were created?

SESSION 6 CLOSING

Closing Song: "This Little Light of Mine,"* The Tune Book, *p. 174a

BENEDICTION

Whatever your gender, whatever your sexual orientation, whatever your gifts and talents, go now and know that you are an equally unique reflection of God's image. Let your light shine and encourage each person to let his or her light also shine.

Disability and Other Diversity Issues

SESSION OPENING WORSHIP

Tips for integrating scripture and worship concepts into Session 7

There are many times during the various exercises in Sessions 6 and 7 when you can lift up how Jesus welcomed and valued all persons, especially those outcast or shunned by others. Read one or two of these stories during the session and repeat the reading during the session closing worship by asking one or two youth to read the stories:

the poor widow (Luke 21:1–4)

the Good Samaritan (Luke 10:29–37)

the sinner who anointed Jesus' feet (Luke 7:36–50)

During the exercises that lift up persons who are differently abled, remind participants of great people in scripture who were also differently abled. Moses was "slow of speech," Leah had "weak eyes," and many scholars believe Paul had some type of physical disability, which he alluded to in some of his letters.

Unit Three Closing Worship

A WORSHIP SERVICE TO CELEBRATE EACH PERSON

Preparing for this worship: Place a large candle in the center of the worship table (in addition to the five candles used in the optional session opening worship). Also put on the table a smaller candle for each participant. The kind many churches use on Christmas Eve would work well. Have everyone stand or sit in a circle around the table. Ask for volunteers to read the various voices in the service.

Song Celebrating the Many Images of God in Which We Are Created:
"Bring Many Names," **The New Century Hymnal #*11***

Scripture Reading: Genesis 1:27 and Galatians 3:28

VOICE ONE: Genesis 1:27 says, "So God created humankind in God's image, in the image of God they were created; male and female they were created!"

ALL: I am created in God's own image!

VOICE TWO: In his letter to the Galatians, Paul wants to put an end to the Galatians' arguing about who is better. He writes, "There is no longer Jew or Greek, there is no longer slave or free, there is no longer male and female; for all of you are one in Christ Jesus."

ALL: We are equal in Christ!

ACKNOWLEDGING OUR LIGHTS AS EQUAL REFLECTIONS OF GOD'S IMAGE

VOICE ONE: We light this candle as a symbol of the image of God.

(Light the large center candle.)

VOICE TWO: Each of us is an equally unique reflection of God's image. I invite you to think of one to five words to describe your unique reflection of that image. It can be your gender, sexual orientation, age, a physical attribute, a gift or talent, or a quality of your personality. We will take a minute in silence for you to decide what you are going to say.

(Allow several moments of silence.)

VOICE THREE: I invite each of you, one at a time, to take one of the smaller candles and light it from the central candle, which symbolizes the image of God. As you light it, lift up to God, either out loud or silently, your words. Then place your lit candle back on the worship table, letting it join its light with others, just as we are joined in worship now. When each person steps back into place, we will all call you by name and say, "You are an equally unique reflection of God's image."

(Go around the circle, allowing each participant to light their candle and share their words. After each has done so:)

ALL: _____, you are an equally unique reflection of God's image.

Closing Song: "This Little Light of Mine,"* The Tune Book, *p. 174a

BENEDICTION

Whatever your gender, whatever your sexual orientation, whatever your gifts and talents, go now and know that you are an equally unique reflection of God's image. Let your light shine and encourage each person to let his or her light also shine.

Sexual Orientation and Gender Identity; Relationships; Lovemaking; and Preparing for Parenthood

A WORD ABOUT WHY THESE UNITS ARE COMBINED

Throughout these sessions, participants explore the significance of relationships. This happens through learning about their own and others' sexual orientation as well as through role playing and experiencing different life experiences and possibilities in the activities. It is important to remind participants that faith has deep importance for our relationships. Our decisions and actions toward others and ourselves are always accountable to God, the faith community, and others. No one acts separate from God or others. In faith, we look to God for the strength to make and keep right decisions and actions.

Key values about relationships are expressed throughout the program and are repeated in the preparation material for Session 15. It would be good to review those values with your group in the opening or closing worships for each of the sessions in these combined units. The key values cannot be repeated often enough! These key values are as important with regard to all our relationships as they are to lovemaking, to which they are initially connected. These values help assure that relationships are positive and life-enhancing experiences when they are

- consensual;
- nonexploitative;
- mutually pleasurable;
- safe;
- developmentally appropriate;
- based on mutual expectations and caring;
- respectful (valuing honesty and keeping commitments).

These units are combined with a closing worship to affirm

- that God is involved in all our relationships;
- that all relationships have value and importance as long as they reflect the key values listed above;
- that we need to respect and be honest with everyone we are in relationship with;
- that we deserve to be respected and cared about by everyone we are in relationship with;
- that there can be elements of healthy sexuality involved in a variety of relationships, not just those in which we are having intercourse.

Sexual Orientation and Gender Identity

SESSION EIGHT

Sexual Orientation

UNIT OPENING WORSHIP

Tips for integrating scripture and worship concepts into Session 8

You will be discussing heterosexual, bisexual, and homosexual orientations in this session. Our culture provides many positive affirmations of heterosexual orientation. This session will affirm all orientations. Most questions will probably be about bisexual and homosexual orientations. The students may have heard negative comments about bisexuality and homosexuality. Because of this, you may find yourself spending more discussion time on these than on heterosexuality.

The United Church of Christ has a long tradition, dating from the late 1960s, of being in the forefront seeking justice for and an end to the social abuse of gay, lesbian, bisexual, and transgender persons. In 1972, our denomination became the first mainline Protestant denomination to ordain an openly gay man, and we have continued since then to welcome into fellowship gay, lesbian, bisexual, and transgender persons.

Some participants may have heard that the Bible is against homosexuality. Detailed biblical exegesis of the topic can be found in *Dirt, Greed and Sex* by L. William Countryman (Philadelphia: Fortress Press, 1988) and in any of James B. Nelson's books on sexuality and embodiment.

In a nutshell, here is what these scholars say about the texts:

- The story of Sodom and Gomorrah (Genesis 19): Instead of homosexuality being the sin, many scholars now say it was the violent intent of the sexuality. This story has nothing to do with a sexual relationship between two consenting adults of the same gender.
- The prohibition in Leviticus (18:22 and 20:13): This was written in a culture that needed all sexual activity to lead to the production of children, preferably sons, to increase the number of members of the tribe. This is not a necessity in our culture. (On a lighter note, the wording used to

prohibit men "lying with other men" is the same wording used to prohibit anyone from touching pig skin, which would rule out most football games.)

- Paul's inclusion of what is translated as homosexuality in his lists of sins (Romans 1:18-27, 1 Corinthians 6:9–10): Many scholars believe that Paul was speaking of a common Greek practice that we would classify as pedophilia, adults having sexual relations with children. Again, this has nothing to do with a sexual relationship between two consenting adults of the same gender.

SESSION 8 CLOSING WORSHIP

Closing Song:* "There Is Someone Somewhere," The Tune Book, *p. 71 (old edition); "Lean on Me,"* The Tune Book, *p. 71 (current edition)

BENEDICTION

Go now and know your sexual orientation is a gift from God, a gift to be cherished and celebrated!

Guest Panel

SESSION OPENING WORSHIP

SESSION CLOSING WORSHIP

Closing Song: ***"There Is Someone Somewhere,"*** **The Tune Book,** ***p. 71 (old edition); "Lean on Me,"*** **The Tune Book,** ***p. 71 (current edition)***

BENEDICTION

Go now and know your sexual orientation is a gift from God, a gift to be cherished and celebrated!

Gender Identity

SESSION OPENING WORSHIP

SESSION CLOSING WORSHIP

Closing Song:* "There Is Someone Somewhere," The Tune Book, *p. 71 (old edition); "Lean on Me,"* The Tune Book, *p. 71 (current edition)

BENEDICTION

Go now and know your sexual orientation is a gift from God, a gift to be cherished and celebrated!

UNIT FIVE

Relationships

SESSION ELEVEN

Introduction to Relationships

UNIT OPENING WORSHIP

Tips for integrating scripture and worship concepts into Session 11

There will be many appropriate times to use examples from scripture as you begin to talk about relationships, friendships, and family.

Problematic family/sibling relationships that were later worked out:

Joseph and his brothers (Genesis 37, 42–47)

the Prodigal Son (Luke 15:11–32)

Family and friends who were very close to one another:

Ruth and her mother-in-law (the Book of Ruth)

David and Jonathan (1 Samuel 18–24, 31 and 2 Samuel 1)

Jesus and Mary, Martha, and Lazarus (John 11)

SESSION 11 CLOSING WORSHIP

Closing Song: "Free to Be Friends,"* The Tune Book, *p. 78b

BENEDICTION

Go now and be a friend as Christ is friend to us all. Go now and cherish your friends as Christ cherishes us all.

Relationship Skills

SESSION OPENING WORSHIP

Tips for integrating scripture and worship concepts into Session 12

There will be many appropriate times to use examples from scripture as you begin to talk about relationships, friendships, and family.

These stories highlight problematic family/sibling relationships that were later worked out. Select two you can read and refer to during the session and that two youth can read during the session Closing Worship:

Joseph and his brothers (Genesis 37, 42–47)

the Prodigal Son (Luke 15:11–32)

Family and friends who were very close to one another:

Ruth and her mother-in-law (the Book of Ruth)

David and Jonathan (1 Samuel 18–24, 31 and 2 Samuel 1)

Jesus and Mary, Martha, and Lazarus (John 11)

SESSION 12 CLOSING WORSHIP

Closing Song: "Free to Be Friends,"* The Tune Book, *p. 78b

BENEDICTION

Go now and be a friend as Christ is friend to us all. Go now and cherish your friends as Christ cherishes us all.

Thorny Issues in Friendship

SESSION OPENING WORSHIP

Tips for integrating scripture and worship concepts into Session 13

There will be many appropriate times to use examples from scripture as you begin to talk about relationships, friendships, and family.

These stories highlight problematic family/sibling relationships that were later worked out. Select two you can read and refer to during the session and two that youth can read during the session Closing Worship:

Joseph and his brothers (Genesis 37, 42–47)

the Prodigal Son (Luke 15:11–32)

Family and friends who were very close to one another:

Ruth and her mother-in-law (the Book of Ruth)

David and Jonathan (1 Samuel 18–24, 31 and 2 Samuel 1)

Jesus and Mary, Martha, and Lazarus (John 11)

SESSION 13 CLOSING WORSHIP

Closing Song: "Free to Be Friends,"* The Tune Book, *p. 78b

BENEDICTION

Go now and be a friend as Christ is friend to us all. Go now and cherish your friends as Christ cherishes us all.

Dating and Lifetime Commitments

SESSION OPENING WORSHIP

Tips for integrating scripture and worship concepts into Session 14

When looking at the elements needed to have a safe, loving relationship, also refer to Paul's words about love in 1 Corinthians 13: Love is patient, kind, etc.

SESSION 14 CLOSING WORSHIP

Closing Song:* "*There Is Someone Somewhere,*" The Tune Book, *p. 71 (old edition); "Lean on Me,"* The Tune Book, *p. 71 (current edition)

BENEDICTION

Go now and know that through the power of God's love, we each can be in relationships where we can share with each other deeply, safely, and joyfully!

UNIT SIX

Lovemaking

SESSION FIFTEEN

Lovemaking Is More than Sex

UNIT OPENING WORSHIP

Tips for integrating scripture and worship concepts into Session 15

Emphasize that love is a gift from God—all kinds of love: the love of friends, the love of family, and the love of lovers. Tell participants that in many places in the Bible a committed sexual relationship is used as a metaphor for God's love of Israel. Let them know that one of the most wonderful books in the Bible, sometimes called the Song of Songs and sometimes, Song of Solomon, is a long, erotic love poem.

SESSION 15 CLOSING WORSHIP

Closing Song: "Oh Mighty God When I Survey in Wonder,"* The New Century Hymnal *#35

BENEDICTION

Go now and live your love for neighbor, self, and God.

Masturbation and Other Sexual Behaviors

SESSION OPENING WORSHIP

Tips for integrating scripture and worship concepts into Session 16

Emphasize that love is a gift from God—all kinds of love: the love of friends, the love of family, and the love of lovers. Tell participants that in many places in the Bible a committed sexual relationship is used as a metaphor for God's love of Israel. Let them know that one of the most wonderful books in the Bible, sometimes called the Song of Songs and sometimes, Song of Solomon, is a long, erotic love poem.

SESSION 16 CLOSING WORSHIP

***Closing Song: "Oh Mighty God When I Survey in Wonder,"* The New Century Hymnal #35**

BENEDICTION

Go now and live your love for neighbor, self, and God.

Preparing for Parenthood

SESSION SEVENTEEN

Conception, Pregnancy, and Birth

UNIT OPENING WORSHIP

Tips for integrating scripture and worship concepts into Session 17

The whole process of conception, pregnancy, and birth is one of the most awesome miracles of God. Genesis 1:27 states that God created us, and we in turn have the ability to be cocreators with God in the creation of other human beings (1:28). This unit is a time to remind participants of that power and of how amazing it is. This is a way both men and women share equally in God's image and creation.

You may want to remind participants that Genesis 1 is just the beginning of the entire Bible, the story of God's involvement with creation and especially with humankind. Just like God, when we are cocreators, we continue to be involved with and responsible for our creation.

Also let them know that Paul speaks of the body as a temple for the Spirit of God (1 Corinthians 3:16–17). In effect, the whole process of planning, conception, pregnancy, and birth are like creating a sacred temple for God's Spirit.

SESSION 17 CLOSING WORSHIP

Closing Song: "Jesus Loves the Little Children," The Tune Book, p. 188a

BENEDICTION

Go now and celebrate the ongoing creation of life!

Teenage Pregnancy

SESSION OPENING WORSHIP

Tips for integrating scripture and worship concepts into Session 18

As you go through Session 18, you may want to remind participants that Mary, Jesus' mother, started out as an unwed, teenage mother. While this is not usually the best option, with the help of God, good things can come out of difficult situations.

The whole process of conception, pregnancy, and birth is one of the most awesome miracles of God. Genesis 1:27 states that God created us and we in turn have the ability to be cocreators with God in the creation of other human beings (1:28). This unit is a time to remind participants of that power and of how amazing it is. This is a way both men and women share equally in God's image and creation.

You may want to remind participants that Genesis 1 is just the beginning of the entire Bible, the story of God's involvement with creation and especially with humankind. Just like God, when we are cocreators, we continue to be involved with and responsible for our creation.

Also let them know that Paul speaks of the body as a temple for the Spirit of God (1 Corinthians 3:16–17). In effect, the whole process of planning, conception, pregnancy, and birth are like creating a sacred temple for God's Spirit.

Units Four Through Seven Closing Worship

A WORSHIP SERVICE TO CELEBRATE ALL OUR RELATIONSHIPS

Preparing for this worship: Place the communion elements on the table. Allow time for participants to make a drawing of someone special in their life. Make sure there is enough room on or around the table for everyone to place their drawings at the appropriate time. Have everyone sit in a circle around the table you use for your opening ritual. Ask for volunteers to read the various voices in this service.

Song Celebrating Relationships (choose one):
"Free to Be Friends," The Tune Book, p. 78b;
"It's a Joy to Get to Know You," The Tune Book, p. 5;
"There Is Someone Somewhere," The Tune Book, p. 71 (old edition);
"Lean on Me," The Tune Book, p. 71 (current edition);
"You've Got a Friend," The Tune Book, p. 9

Scripture Readings about Relationships: Various Selections

VOICE ONE: In Genesis 45, when Joseph and all his brothers were reunited, Joseph said, "'Hurry and bring my father down here.' Then he fell upon his brother Benjamin's neck and wept, while Benjamin wept upon his neck. And he kissed all his brothers and wept upon them."

VOICE TWO: The Book of Ruth relates how deeply Ruth loved her mother-in-law. In the first chapter, Ruth says to her mother-in-law, "Do not press me to leave you or to turn back from following you! Where you go, I will go; where you lodge, I will lodge; your people shall be my people, and your God my God."

VOICE THREE: In 1 Samuel, we hear of the love Jonathan and David had for each other. In chapter 20, after Jonathan shared with David a plan to keep David safe, "Jonathan made David swear again by his love for him; for he loved him as he loved his own life."

VOICE FOUR: The Song of Solomon celebrates romantic love and passion as the lovers describe and speak to each other. One says, "Kiss me with the kisses of [your] mouth! For your love is better than wine,...your name is perfume poured out." The other says, "Set me as a seal upon your heart, as a seal upon your arm; for love is strong as death, passion fierce as the grave. Its flashes are flashes of fire, a raging flame. Many waters cannot quench love, neither can floods drown it."

VOICE FIVE: In the Gospel of John, chapter 15, Jesus says, "This is my commandment, that you love one another as I have loved you. No one has greater love than this, to lay down one's life for one's friends."

SHARING IN THE MEAL THAT REMINDS US OF OUR RELATIONSHIPS

VOICE ONE: Jesus had family that he loved and struggled with, friends he cared about deeply—many very human relationships like the ones we have. At the end of his life, when he knew he was going to die, he gathered together those closest to him to share a meal with them. Sharing a meal is still a way we spend time with those we are in relationship with.

VOICE TWO: And so today we share a meal with each other and also celebrate our special relationships. I invite each of you to come forward and place the drawing of someone special in your life on the table before you take communion. Through communion, we are reminded that everyone is welcome at God's table, regardless of gender, sexual orientation, or family status.

CELEBRANT: Jesus took the bread, the same kind of bread they had eaten so many times before, and broke it and said, "Take, eat; this is my body broken for you. Whenever you do this, do it in remembrance of me." In the same way he took the cup, filled with the same wine they had drunk together so many times, and said, "Take, drink; this is the cup of the new covenant. Whenever you drink from it, do so in remembrance of me."

ALL: We each have many relationships. Some are easy; some are full of struggle. Some are strong; some are broken, like the bread. As we eat this bread and drink from this cup, let us celebrate all our relationships.

(Each person can go to the table, place their picture on it and partake of communion.)

***Closing Song: "I Come with Joy,"* The New Century Hymnal #349**

BENEDICTION

Go now and celebrate all your relationships!

Responsible Sexual Behavior; Sexually Transmitted Diseases; and Abuse of Sexuality

A WORD ABOUT WHY THESE UNITS ARE COMBINED

These units are combined with a closing worship to affirm

- that all issues are interconnected in very complex ways and
- that God loves us whatever choices and decisions we make.

Responsible Sexual Behavior

SESSION NINETEEN

Defining/Redefining Abstinence

UNIT OPENING WORSHIP

Tips for integrating scripture and worship concepts into Session 19

This unit is about decisions. The closing worship service for this group of units (Units Eight through Ten) ends with the participants covenanting with God to express their sexuality in healthy ways. It invites them to remember that if they do make mistakes, God can give them the strength to face the natural consequences of their choices. It is important to stress that sexuality and sexual behavior are part of how God created us. You can again allude to that wonderful erotic love poem in the Hebrew Scriptures, the Song of Songs (Song of Solomon). God does not expect us to deny our sexuality but to express it responsibly.

SESSION 19 CLOSING WORSHIP

***Closing Song:* *"I Would Be True," v. 1,* The New Century Hymnal #492**

BENEDICTION

Go now and, with the help of God, make healthy decisions about how you express your sexuality.

Contraception

SESSION OPENING WORSHIP

Tips for integrating scripture and worship concepts into Session 20

This unit is about decisions. The Closing Worship for this group of units (Units Eight through Ten) ends with the participants covenanting with God to express their sexuality in healthy ways. It invites them to remember that if they do make mistakes, God can give them the strength to face the natural consequences of their choices. It is important to stress that sexuality and sexual behavior are part of how God created us. You can again allude to that wonderful erotic love poem in the Hebrew Scriptures, the Song of Songs (Song of Solomon). God does not expect us to deny our sexuality but to express it responsibly.

SESSION 20 CLOSING WORSHIP

***Closing Song: "I Would Be True," v. 1,* The New Century Hymnal #492**

BENEDICTION

Go now and, with the help of God, make healthy decisions about how you express your sexuality.

Unintended Pregnancy Options

SESSION OPENING WORSHIP

Tips for integrating scripture and worship concepts into Session 21

Choice is an important concept in this unit. The idea that both healthy and unhealthy choices in sexuality have consequences is also important. The Closing Worship uses the passage from Deuteronomy (30:19) about choosing life that has been interpreted very narrowly by the anti-abortion movement. A much broader interpretation is used in this worship: We are free to choose to act in ways that bring about a healthy life or an unhealthy life that can even lead to death. This interpretation acknowledges that there are situations in which choosing to have an abortion may be the best choice.

This unit is also about decisions. The closing worship service for this group of units (Units Eight through Ten) ends with the participants covenanting with God to express their sexuality in healthy ways. It invites them to remember that if they do make mistakes, God can give them the strength to face the natural consequences of their choices. It is important to stress that sexuality and sexual behavior are part of how God created us. You can again allude to that wonderful erotic love poem in the Hebrew Scriptures, the Song of Songs (Song of Solomon). God does not expect us to deny our sexuality but to express it responsibly.

SESSION 21 CLOSING WORSHIP

Closing Song: "I Would Be True," v. 1, **The New Century Hymnal #492**

BENEDICTION

Go now and, with the help of God, make healthy decisions about how you express your sexuality.

Sexual Decisions

SESSION OPENING WORSHIP

Tips for integrating scripture and worship concepts into Session 22

This unit is about decisions. The closing worship service for this group of units (Units Eight through Ten) ends with the participants covenanting with God to express their sexuality in healthy ways. It invites them to remember that if they do make mistakes, God can give them the strength to face the natural consequences of their choices. It is important to stress that sexuality and sexual behavior are part of how God created us. You can again allude to that wonderful erotic love poem in the Hebrew Scriptures, the Song of Songs (Song of Solomon). God does not expect us to deny our sexuality but to express it responsibly.

SESSION 22 CLOSING WORSHIP

Closing Song: "I Would Be True," v. 1, **The New Century Hymnal #492**

BENEDICTION

Go now and, with the help of God, make healthy decisions about how you express your sexuality.

Sexually Transmitted Diseases (STDs)

SESSION TWENTY-THREE

STD Facts

UNIT OPENING WORSHIP

Tips for integrating scripture and worship concepts into Session 23

Throughout this unit, you will be talking about specific behavior that may or may not result in contracting an STD. Remind participants that their bodies are sacred temples for God's Spirit (1 Corinthians 3:16–17). They have a responsibility to express their sexuality in ways that keep them healthy physically, emotionally, and spiritually.

It is also important to stress that those who have an STD are still loved and cherished by God. Nothing can separate us from the love of God (Romans 8:38–39). It is not our place to judge persons who have an STD. "Do not judge, so that you may not be judged" (Matthew 7:1).

SESSION 23 CLOSING WORSHIP

***Closing Song: "I Would Be True," v. 1,* The New Century Hymnal #492**

BENEDICTION

Go now and, with the help of God, make healthy decisions about how you express your sexuality.

STD Prevention

SESSION OPENING WORSHIP

Tips for integrating scripture and worship concepts into Session 24

Throughout this unit, you will be talking about specific behavior that may or may not result in contracting an STD. Remind participants that their bodies are sacred temples for God's Spirit (1 Corinthians 3:16–17) and that they have a responsibility to express their sexuality in ways that keep them healthy physically, emotionally, and spiritually.

It is also important to stress that those who have an STD are still loved and cherished by God. Nothing can separate us from the love of God (Romans 8:38–39). It is not our place to judge persons who have an STD. "Do not judge, so that you may not be judged" (Matthew 7:1).

SESSION 24 CLOSING WORSHIP

***Closing Song: "I Would Be True," v. 1,* The New Century Hymnal #492**

BENEDICTION

Go now and, with the help of God, make healthy decisions about how you express your sexuality.

Abuse of Sexuality

SESSION TWENTY-FIVE

Recovering from Sexual Abuse

UNIT OPENING WORSHIP

Tips for integrating scripture and worship concepts into Session 25

One of the first things to stress in this session is that the victims of sexual violence are not somehow being punished by God. Whenever sexual violence happens, God's heart is the first to break in grief. As stated in the tips for Session Eight, many scholars now believe that the destruction of Sodom and Gomorrah was brought about by sexual violence. Scripture may also record the deep anger and sorrow of someone who has been sexually abused, harassed, or raped. Reread Psalm 6, one of the psalms of lament and grief, with that in mind.

Scripture was written in a culture in which women, male and female children, and male and female slaves were considered property. Yet even in this cultural context, there were strong prohibitions against incest and rape. (See, for example, the long lists in Leviticus 18 and Deuteronomy 22 and 23.) Some of these laws may seem strange to our modern sensibilities. At the time, however, many of them were a leap forward, especially in the treatment of women, children, and slaves. The same can be said for Paul's statements about marriage (Ephesians 5:22–33). At that time, it was expected that women would be subject to their husbands. The radical surprise is that Paul goes on to say, “In the same way, husbands should love their wives as they do their own bodies.” It is not okay for men to abuse their wives.

Jesus is the best example of someone who treated people equally and who treated women, men, and children as if they were persons and not property. Remember Jesus' interactions with the sinful woman who anointed his feet (Luke 7:36–50) and the Samaritan woman at the well who had lived with many men (John 4:1–42). In John 8:1–11, Jesus saves from stoning a woman caught in adultery. Perhaps he understood the complex reasons people find themselves in those situations.

SESSION 25 CLOSING WORSHIP

A WORSHIP SERVICE TO ACKNOWLEDGE HUMAN PAIN AND TO PRAY FOR HEALING

Preparing for this worship: Set up a low table in the center of the room. Cover it with broken pieces of dishes, pottery, or toys, and torn and tattered fabric. Put five candles on the table and light them. (These may be the same five candles used in the optional session opening worship.) Have close by something with which to extinguish the candles during the litany, and matches or a lighter to relight them during the closing song. Make sure at least two people know the closing song so they can lead the singing. Ask for volunteers to read the various voices in this service.

Song Acknowledging God's Presence in Times of Pain (choose one):
"O Christ, the Healer, We Have Come,"* The New Century Hymnal *#175;
"Amazing Grace, How Sweet the Sound,"* The New Century Hymnal *#547;
"O God, My God,"* The New Century Hymnal *#515

A Litany to Remember Those in Pain and to Pray for Healing

VOICE ONE: Every day someone is told that he or she is ugly. Every day someone is told that he or she is stupid. Every day someone is told that he or she is worthless.

(Extinguish one of the candles on the table.)

VOICE ONE: Hear us now, God, as we lift up to you, either out loud or silently, the names of those we know who have suffered this. After each name is spoken, let the people say, "Heal us, O God."

(If no one speaks, let the group sit in silence for 20 to 30 seconds.)

VOICE TWO: Every 15 minutes a woman is raped. One in seven boys is molested by the time he reaches age 16. Every day someone's sexual health is assaulted and violated.

(Extinguish one of the candles on the table.)

VOICE TWO: Hear us now, God, as we lift up to you, either out loud or silently, the names of those we know who have suffered this. After each name is spoken, let the people say, "Heal us, O God."

(If no one speaks, let the group sit in silence for 20 to 30 seconds.)

VOICE THREE: Hundreds of children are born each year to people who cannot care for them or who do not want them. The fastest growing area of new HIV cases is young people in their twenties who contracted the disease in their teens by not practicing safe sex. Everywhere, there are people who do not take responsibility for their own sexuality.

(Extinguish one of the candles on the table.)

VOICE THREE: Hear us now, God, as we lift up to you, either out loud or silently, the names of those we know who have suffered this. After each name is spoken, let the people say, "Heal us, O God."

(If no one speaks, let the group sit in silence for 20 to 30 seconds.)

VOICE FOUR: Each day thousands of people are subjected to sexist remarks or jokes. Every day a man or boy is made fun of because he does not act like the stereotypical male. In schools and workplaces around the world, people are sexually harassed. The battle continues to rage in our society over reproductive rights. Justice is not served.

(Extinguish one of the candles on the table.)

VOICE FOUR: Hear us now, God, as we lift up to you, either out loud or silently, the names of those we know who have suffered this. After each name is spoken, let the people say, "Heal us, O God."

(If no one speaks, let the group sit in silence for 20 to 30 seconds.)

VOICE FIVE: In cities and towns all over the world, gay and lesbian people are harassed and discriminated against because of their sexual orientation. Still, in this time in history, mixed race couples are harassed. People in wheelchairs and with other physical or mental challenges are treated as if they have no sexuality.

(Extinguish one of the candles on the table.)

VOICE FIVE: Hear us now, God, as we lift up to you, either out loud or silently, the names of those we know who have suffered this. After each name is spoken, let the people say, "Heal us, O God."

(If no one speaks, let the group sit in silence for 20 to 30 seconds.)

Closing Song of Hope and Solidarity: "I Am One Voice" by Don Eaton (p. 174 of this volume)

(Relight a candle after each verse.)

BENEDICTION

God, give us the strength to work for the self-worth of all your people, to work for the sexual health of all your people, to take responsibility for our own sexuality, to work for justice, and to strive to be inclusive of all your people.

I Am One Voice

Words & Music by
Don Eaton

Sexual Harassment and Acquaintance Rape

SESSION OPENING WORSHIP

Tips for integrating scripture and worship concepts into Session 26

One of the first things to stress in this session is that the victims of sexual violence are not somehow being punished by God. Whenever sexual violence happens, God's heart is the first to break in grief. As stated in the tips for Session Eight, many scholars now believe that the destruction of Sodom and Gomorrah was brought about by sexual violence. Scripture may also record the deep anger and sorrow of someone who has been sexually abused, harassed, or raped. Reread Psalm 6, one of the psalms of lament and grief, with that in mind.

Scripture was written in a culture where women, male and female children, and male and female slaves were considered property. Yet even in this cultural context, there were strong prohibitions against incest and rape. (See, for example, the long lists in Leviticus 18 and Deuteronomy 22 and 23.) Some of these laws may seem strange to our modern sensibilities. At the time, however, many of them were a leap forward, especially in the treatment of women, children, and slaves. The same can be said for Paul's statements about marriage (Ephesians 5:22–33). At that time, it was expected that women would be subject to their husbands. The radical surprise is that Paul goes on to say, "In the same way, husbands should love their wives as they do their own bodies." It is not okay for people to abuse their partners. When abuse occurs, marriage vows are broken and relationships are violated. It is the right and loving thing to do to leave an abusive relationship.

Jesus is the best example of someone who treated people equally and who treated women, men, and children as if they were persons and not property. Remember Jesus' interactions with the sinful woman who anointed his feet (Luke 7:36–50) and the Samaritan woman at the well who had lived with many men (John 4:1–42). In John 8:1–11, Jesus saves from stoning a woman caught in adultery. Perhaps he understood the complex reasons people find themselves in those situations.

Units Eight Through Ten Closing Worship

A WORSHIP SERVICE TO COVENANT WITH GOD ABOUT RESPONSIBLE DECISION MAKING IN SEXUALITY

Preparing for this worship: Have a covenant card for each participant, including the adult leadership. Ask for volunteers to read the various voices in this service.

***Song of Covenanting: "I Would Be True,"* The New Century Hymnal #492**

Scripture Readings About Deciding to Express Our Sexuality in Healthy Ways: Genesis 1:27, 1 Corinthians 3:16–17, Deuteronomy 30:19, and Romans 8:38–39

VOICE ONE: We have the ability to make decisions to express our sexuality in healthy ways because we remember that Genesis 1:27 says we were created in the image of God.

VOICE TWO: "So God created humankind in God's own image, in the image of God they were created; male and female they were created."

ALL: We have the ability to make healthy decisions.

VOICE THREE: We have the responsibility to make decisions to express our sexuality in healthy ways because we read in 1 Corinthians 3:16–17 that our spiritual physical beings are sacred temples of God.

VOICE FOUR: "Do you not know that you are God's temple and that God's Spirit dwells in you?...For God's temple is holy, and you are that temple."

ALL: We have the responsibility to make healthy decisions.

VOICE ONE: We have the choice to make decisions to express our sexuality in healthy ways. We can choose to express our sexuality in ways that lead to a healthy life, or we can choose to express our sexuality in ways that lead to physical and emotional sickness and even to death.

VOICE TWO: "I have set before you life and death, blessings and curses. Choose life so that you and your descendants may live."

ALL: We have the choice to make healthy decisions.

VOICE THREE: If we decide to express our sexuality in unhealthy ways, we may also have to deal with the consequences of that decision—a broken heart, hurting another person, an unwanted pregnancy, a physical illness, perhaps even death. Yet God still loves us and, if we ask, will give us the strength to face those consequences and the opportunity to make more healthy choices in the future. Paul writes in Romans 8:38–39:

VOICE FOUR: "For I am convinced that neither death, nor life, nor angels, nor rulers, nor things present, nor things to come, nor powers, nor height, nor depth, nor anything else in all creation, will be able to separate us from the love of God in Christ Jesus our Lord."

ALL: We have the love of God no matter what our decisions.

COVENANTING WITH GOD TO EXPRESS OUR SEXUALITY IN HEALTHY WAYS

(Distribute covenant cards to each person.)

VOICE ONE: A covenant is a promise we make with ourselves and with God. You are now invited to look at the covenant card and to carefully reflect on your decision making. When you have prayed about it, fill out the promises you are ready to make and sign your card. When everyone is finished, we will ask God's blessing on you and your card. These promises are confidential—a covenant between you and God; you don't have to show your card to anyone. We invite you to keep it with you or in a place you will see it every day to remind you of your covenant.

(Allow time for prayer and filling out the cards.)

VOICE TWO: We invite you to hold your card against your heart and close your eyes. Let us pray: God, who made us in your image, whose Spirit dwells in our bodies, who created us with free will, and who promises us your unconditional love, bless us now in the covenant we make with you this day. Give us the strength to keep this covenant and hold us in your love.

Closing Song: "Wonder of Wonders, Here Revealed," v. 1,* The New Century Hymnal *#328

BENEDICTION

Go now and, with the help of God, make healthy decisions about how you express your sexuality.

Covenant Card

I make this covenant (sacred promise) with God:

_________ to express my sexuality in ways that lead to my physical, emotional, spiritual, and sexual health;

_________ to make my own decisions and not to let someone else pressure me into doing something I do not want to do;

_________ to affirm justice and diversity in regard to sexuality;

_________ to ask for God's help with the consequences when I make a mistake and to know that God continues to love me no matter what I do.

Signature Date

Conclusion

SESSION TWENTY-SEVEN

Celebration and Closure

CLOSING WORSHIP FOR THE PROGRAM

This service mirrors the opening worship for the curriculum. In that worship, participants had the opportunity to take vows to explore, grow, and learn about what it means to be spiritual physical beings expressing their sexuality in healthy ways. This service commissions them to continue this lifelong process.

Preparing for this worship: In the center of the room, set up a low table covered with brightly colored fabric. Place five candles in holders on the table. Have matches or a lighter handy. Ask for volunteers to read the various voices in this service.

Each participant, including leaders, will be commissioned near the end of the worship, so you will need strips of plain cloth to use as stoles and markers to write on them. Before the service starts, have each person take a stole and write their name on it. Then have them draw on it a symbol that represents themselves, another symbol that represents other people, and something that represents God and the Body of Christ. Finally, have the participants draw lines to connect all three symbols.

Gathering Chant: The New Century Hymnal #742

Call to Worship

(Have someone light a candle as each of the program values is lifted up.)

VOICE ONE: Why have we come together?

ALL: We come to worship God in whose image we were created—spiritual physical beings.

VOICE ONE: God gifted us with bodies and emotions to express our spirituality in concrete ways. One of the ways we affirm the sacredness of life is through healthy sexuality.

ALL: Let us celebrate God's gift of incarnation and affirm our desire for sexual health and the joy it brings.

(Light a candle.)

VOICE TWO: In the beginning, God gave humanity life and blessed us. God continues to bless each of us individually.

ALL: Let us celebrate God's gift and remember our own self-worth.

(Light a candle.)

VOICE TWO: God gifted us with free will—the ability to make our own decisions.

ALL: Let us celebrate God's guidance and help as we struggle with this wonderful and awesome responsibility.

(Light a candle.)

VOICE ONE: The God in whose image we are created is a God of justice.

ALL: Let us answer that call for justice in our own lives and relationships.

(Light a candle.)

VOICE TWO: The God in whose image we are created is a God of diversity.

ALL: Let us celebrate that diversity by working to include all people, regardless of their gender, physical differences, sexual orientation, age, race, and other things that make us different from one another.

(Light a candle.)

VOICE ONE: Let us pray:

ALL: God of touch and taste, sight and sound, aromas and delight, thank you for giving us the breath of life. Thank you for your blessings on us as fully human beings. Help us to use our gifts as we work with you to bring more joy and justice into your world. Help us to delight in our differences and to welcome each other into this amazing world you created for us. Amen.

Song Celebrating Our Being Part of the Body of Christ: "Many Are the Lightbeams," **The New Century Hymnal** *#163*

Scripture Reading: Romans 12:4–8 and 1 Corinthians 12:12–13

VOICE ONE: We live out our spirituality in sacred bodies, and together we are the Body of Christ. Hear how the apostle Paul describes it in Romans:

VOICE TWO: "For as in one body we have many members, and not all the members have the same function, so we, who are many, are one body in Christ, and individually we are members one of another."

VOICE THREE: "We have gifts that differ according to the grace given to us: prophecy, in proportion to faith; ministry, in ministering; the teacher, in teaching; the exhorter, in exhortation; the giver, in generosity; the leader, in diligence; the compassionate, in cheerfulness."

VOICE ONE: And in I Corinthians 12:12–13, Paul writes:

VOICE TWO: "For just as the body is one and has many members, and all the members of the body, though many, are one body, so it is with Christ. For in the one Spirit we were all baptized into one body—Jews or Greeks, slaves or free—and we were all made to drink of one Spirit."

COMMISSIONING PARTICIPANTS TO CONTINUE EXPLORING WHAT IT MEANS TO BE SPIRITUAL PHYSICAL BEINGS

VOICE ONE: Today we remember the vows we took at the beginning of this program and decide if we want to continue them in our future. Throughout this program, we have explored and learned about many topics. Will you promise to continue to listen to your own thoughts and words as you continue to explore what you think and believe and, in so doing, learn more about yourself?

(Allow a few moments of silence while participants decide if they can commit to that.)

VOICE ONE: If you are willing, please respond:

PARTICIPANTS (including adults): I will, with the help of God.

Voice Two: Will you promise to continue to listen to the ideas and thoughts of others and, in so doing, learn about others?

(Allow a few moments of silence while each participant decides if they can commit to that.)

VOICE TWO: If you are willing, please respond:

PARTICIPANTS (including adults): I will, with the help of God.

VOICE THREE: We are sacred, spiritual physical beings. Everything we do with our bodies is an opportunity to show, in a concrete way, the image of God in which we were created and to show that we are part of the Body of Christ. Will you promise to look for those connections throughout your life?

(Allow a few moments of silence while participants decide if they can commit to that.)

VOICE THREE: If you are willing, please respond:

PARTICIPANTS (including adults): I will, with the help of God.

VOICE ONE: Let us pray.

ALL: God, thank you for making us in your image. Thank you for making us part of the Body of Christ. Help us keep our promises as we learn more about ourselves, each other, you, and especially who we are as sacred, spiritual physical beings. Amen.

VOICE TWO: Take your stole and turn to a partner. Have your partner place your stole around your neck and say, "You are commissioned to continue exploring what it means to be a spiritual physical being."

***Closing Song: "Blessed Be the Tie That Binds," v. 1,* The New Century Hymnal #393**

BENEDICTION

Go now and learn, listen, explore, and grow!

Sexuality Education Curriculum Components

Our Whole Lives: Sexuality Education for Grades K-1
by Barbara Sprung. Eight one-hour sessions.

Sexuality and Our Faith: A Companion to Our Whole Lives Grades K-1
Unitarian Universalist: by Rev. Patricia Hoertdoerfer and Rev. Makanah Elizabeth Morriss
United Church of Christ: by Rev. John M. Barrett and Faith Adams Johnson

Our Whole Lives: Sexuality Education for Grades 4-6
by Elizabeth M. Casparian, Ph.D, and Eva S. Goldfarb, Ph.D. Eight one-hour sessions.

To be used with: *It's Perfectly Normal: Changing Bodies, Growing Up, Sex and Sexual Health*, by Robie Harris, illustrated by Michael Emberley, Candlewick Press, 1994.

Sexuality and Our Faith: A Companion to Our Whole Lives Grades 4-6
Unitarian Universalist: by Rev. Patricia Hoertdoerfer and Rev. Makanah Elizabeth Morriss
United Church of Christ: by Rev. John M. Barrett and Faith Adams Johnson

The Parent Guide to Our Whole Lives Grades K-1 and Grades 4-6
by Rev. Patricia Hoertdoerfer

Our Whole Lives: Sexuality Education for Grades 7-9
by Pamela M. Wilson, MSW. Twenty-seven ninety-minute sessions.

Sexuality and Our Faith: A Companion to Our Whole Lives Grades 7-9
Unitarian Universalist: by Rev. Makanah Elizabeth Morriss and Rev. Jory Agate
United Church of Christ: by Rev. Lizann Bassham and Rev. Gordon J. Svoboda II

Slides to accompany religious supplements to *Our Whole Lives Grades 7-9*. Black and white drawings. Script and discussion guide included.

Our Whole Lives: Sexuality Education for Grades 10-12
by Eva S. Goldfarb, Ph.D. and Elizabeth M. Casparian, Ph.D. Twelve two-hour sessions.

Sexuality and Our Faith: A Companion to Our Whole Lives Grades 10-12
Unitarian Universalist: by Rev. Makanah Elizabeth Morriss, Rev. Jory Agate, and Sarah Gibb
United Church of Christ: by Rev. Lizann Bassham and Rev. Gordon J. Svoboda II

Video to accompany religious supplements to *Our Whole Lives Grades 10-12*. Script by Eva S. Goldfarb, Ph.D. and Elizabeth M. Casparian, Ph.D. Produced by Mark Schoen, Ph.D.

Our Whole Lives: Sexuality Education for Adults
by Richard S. Kimball. Fourteen two-hour sessions.

Sexuality and Our Faith: A Companion to Our Whole Lives for Adults
Unitarian Universalist: by Judith A. Frediani

The Advocacy Manual for Sexuality Education, Health and Justice: Resources for Communities of Faith
Sarah Gibb, editor